M000214988

The Midas Method

by
Stuart G Goldsmith

Illustrated by

Lisa Henley

First Published 1988
Re-printed 1989
Re-printed 1991
Re-printed 1992
Re-printed 1993

Copyright Stuart Goldsmith 1988, 1989, 1990, 1991, 1992,1993

All rights reserved.
No reproduction without the
prior permission of the publishers.

MEDINA LTD
70 Southview Ave
Caversham
Reading
Berkshire
RG4 0HO

Printed and bound in Great Britain
by Redwood Books, Trowbridge, Wiltshire

Typesetting (in Times Roman 9pt) by
CHEVRON COMPUTER TYPESETTERS LTD

ISBN 1 871379 00 8

CONTENTS

A NEW START

1

This book is about belief. Believing in yourself. Believing that you *can* have more, that you *deserve* more.

A few years ago, I didn't believe. I didn't believe in myself enough to get the things that I really wanted. I thought that those things were for other people – a nice house, a good quality car. At best I thought (if I did think about it at all), that one day, at some distant, undefined time in the future, I might have a few of those things. But not many.

I was jogging along, working for a major U.K. Corporation, underpaid and with no hope of promotion. I was renting a flat and driving a beaten-up old car which would hardly pass its road-worthiness test.

My love-life was a mess and my bank balance was very red.

Financially I was just holding my life together; the same as most people.

I received weekly letters from the bank demanding repayment of my unauthorised overdraft. There was no hope of promotion at work, and hence no hope of a salary increase.

I was also enmeshed in a deeply unhappy relationship from which I couldn't seem to escape.

Does this story sound a bit like yours? At least in places?

Don't worry, there are millions of people in this country with a very similar tale to tell.

About this time, someone sold me a 'Positive Thinking' book. I don't remember the title, but I do remember that when I read it I was very sceptical.

That book had a very simple message. The message was this:

BELIEVE THAT YOU CAN DO SOMETHING AND YOU WILL DO IT

This sounded so ridiculously simple, that my first reaction was to laugh it off, and forget the money that I had spent on that book. But something kept nagging away at me; I couldn't seem to get that simple message out of my mind. I ended up reading the book several times over.

The idea was so simple; yet it had a ring of truth about it. Could it really be so easy? Was there a way that I could apply this principle and improve my *own* circumstances?

After reading and re-reading that book, I decided that I had nothing to lose. It wasn't actually going to *cost* me anything to try this idea. I wasn't being asked to send in any more money or invest capital in a 'Get Rich Quick' scheme; I was merely being asked to *believe*; to have faith in myself. I figured that it couldn't be a bad thing to have faith in myself, regardless of whether or not I got rich at the end of it.

I also knew that if these principles could work for me, then they could work for anyone; because I had almost nothing! I was in exactly the same situation as most people. If, by putting these principles to work, I could start from nothing and get even a fraction of the things that I wanted, then I must be onto a winner!

From that moment on, there was no stopping me. I read every book about 'Positive Thinking' that was going. Some were terrible, some were very good; but all were lacking in something.

Even at this early stage, before I had applied the principles of 'Positive Thinking'; I thought to myself, "If this works, I'm going to write my own book and pass on my experiences." In a sense I was using myself as a guinea-pig. If these principles could work for me; they could work for anyone!

What Did I Do?

During the following months, I put together my own system of success through Positive Thinking, (this is the Midas Method, the system which I am going to share with you in this book). I then put that system to work, using myself as a human guinea-pig. I made a lot of mistakes in those early months, but gradually I evolved a system which started to bring unbelievable results for me. When I first realised the potential of this system, I felt as though I had discovered a secret formula, a formula which, if it worked, could lead to huge success for me; and if it failed...well, I wouldn't have lost much.

Over the next few years I fine-tuned the Midas Method to bring HUGE personal benefits for myself, I felt as though everything I touched turned to gold!

The Result?

It took me eight years. Now I drive the car I want, (a BMW worth £22,000.) I live in a house worth £250,000, (with a small mortgage for tax reasons), and my net assets are in excess of one million pounds.

That's not bad going for eight years is it?

But I think that's a *long* time! Remember, I was developing the Midas Method as I went along; you don't have to do this. I will hand you the method on a plate! You won't have to waste valuable time developing a system from scratch like I did – you could achieve your goals in far less time if you wanted to.

How Did I Do It?

Now this is the important point. I want you to trust me and believe what I am now going to tell you:

I achieved my million pounds (and all the other things), by using my own system which I call the Midas Method. This is the system outlined in this book. I did not, (as in a lot of 'Get Rich Quick' books), have a helping hand up from anyone.

Nobody left me a penny. I have no special talents or abilities, (although I have my fair share, just like you). I wasn't 'lucky' in the sense that I discovered that my house was built on an oil well, or that I gambled money and won. I've had my fair share of good and bad luck over the last eight years – just like you.

Starting with a large overdraft, I achieved everything that I have today by simply changing my beliefs. By believing that I *deserved* these things. By believing that it wasn't just other people who made money or got the good things in life – by believing that I could do it if I really wanted to. That's all. It's that simple. This is the only major 'secret' I am going to impart to you in this book.

The rest of the book is devoted to *convincing you* that what I say is true.

Why do I need to convince you? Because if you genuinely believed what I said, you would already be well on the way to having everything you wanted. You would not need this book, and you probably would not have bought it.

The very fact that you are reading this book means that you probably don't have everything you really want. I'm telling you that the main thing stopping you from having everything that you really want is BELIEF. You *can* have it if you believe that you deserve it.

What this book does is to batter away at your disbelief and scepticism until you are at least at the point where you will *try* my system. If you will only trust me enough to *try*, then I'll lead you step-by-step to the stage where you won't need faith that what I say is true; you will *know* for yourself. How? Because I guarantee results every step of the way. By getting positive results – by seeing the system working – you will start to believe.

It's this step-by-step approach which makes the Midas Method so effective. Why? Because you get *results* every step of the way. You can see the system working with your own eyes and you are not asked to accept too much on blind faith.

For example, take the following statement:

BELIEVE IN YOURSELF AND YOU CAN HAVE AS MUCH MONEY AS YOU DESIRE.

Do you believe this statement? The chances are that you don't (at this stage). So what would be the point in me telling you to recite this over and over again until you believed it? You wouldn't! You would just get bored and give up; then you would put this book on the bookshelf and forget it! That's not what I want.

I want you to succeed. I want you to have all the things you deserve. I achieved everything I ever wanted by using this system and this system alone. Don't let your scepticism and disbelief stand between you and success.

Harmful Beliefs

You probably believe (quite strongly) that there are all sorts of things standing between you and a large amount of money. (I use money as an example, you might want something else.)

You probably *believe* that all or some of these things stand in your way:

1) Age: ("I'm too old/young.")
2) Sex: ("It's tough if you're a woman/man.")
3) Background: ("I never had a chance.")
4) Physical abilities: ("With my wooden leg? Forget it!")
5) Luck: ("I never get the breaks.")
6) Education: ("I was in my first job at thirteen.")
7) Race: ("It's hard if you're Black/Chinese/Asian etc.")

If you hold such strong beliefs (and the chances are that you hold at least a few of these); I would be wasting my breath just telling you that you are wrong!

You will only change your belief if I give you the *evidence* to allow you to change your belief.

My step-by-step approach gives you the evidence you need to prove that the Midas Method works. Armed with the evidence, you will then believe in the system.

This is where all the other systems go wrong. They ask you for too much faith, too early. The result is that people get bored and give up.

They might try the system a few times out of curiosity, or, if they are particularly diligent and hard-working, they might try for a few weeks, but the end result is the same for most people – they give up.

Perhaps that is what the authors intend; that way no-one asks for their money back!

The Midas Method leads you step-by-step through a series of exercises which prove beyond doubt that belief can indeed work wonders. In fact I guarantee results – fast, and every step of the way.

You will be given a series of small, achievable tasks and be asked to apply the system to them. These tasks will easily bring results in weeks or even days. When you have proved (to yourself), that the Midas Method works for these small tasks, then you will move onto larger goals.

If you follow my instructions faithfully, I guarantee that the results will be little short of miraculous!

Starting from NOTHING, I obtained a MILLION POUNDS using only the secrets divulged to you in this book. I obtained a great many more things besides. For example, I only work two or three days a week 'making money', the rest of the time is mine to do with as I please – I don't have to work at all if I don't feel like it!

If I can do this, starting with an overdraft, I KNOW that you can – because there is nothing 'special' about me. It's all very well if someone tells you how they made a million after 'Daddy' left them half a million! Anyone could do that! It is also interesting, but irrelevant, if someone who is a brilliant inventor, or a financial genius, makes a million. Good for them! But where does that leave the *ordinary* person like you and I?

If you are in anything like the position I was in, then you'll probably have almost no spare money (perhaps a few hundred if you sell some things!) and you probably are not absolutely brilliant at any one thing. You are exactly the sort of person this book is aimed at. Forgive me for categorising you, but I wrote this book for the normal, ordinary person who has a genuine desire to obtain everything they have ever wanted. It CAN be done; I know, because I did it!

You are on your way to an exciting new life. A life where you can achieve ALL of the things you want to achieve; where wealth, success and happiness are within *your* grasp. Will you reach out with me now and take them?

THE SECRET OF SUCCESS

2

There are four steps to attaining everything that you want in life. They are simple steps and I will tell you what they are:-

1. **Know what you want.**
2. **Believe that you are worth it.**
3. **Believe that you can achieve it.**
4. **Go out and get it.**

Now; (and this is surprising part of the system), most people would think that item number four – getting what you want – is the biggest obstacle standing in their path. THEY WOULD BE WRONG!

You will be surprised to learn that *knowing what you want* and *believing that you can get it,* form over SEVENTY-FIVE PERCENT of the secret of success. Yes, 75%!

Actually going out and getting the things you desire is only 25% of the battle!

You, like me, and millions of other people, have probably spent a lifetime thinking that it was the other way round! You probably thought that belief in yourself and knowing what you want formed 25% of the solution, and that getting the things you want formed 75%. This is the first of many 'minor secrets' which I will impart to you in this book.

Believe me, it makes a big difference knowing that your mental attitude is responsible for 75% of the obstacles standing between you and success. When I first realised this, it was as though a cloud had lifted from my vision. I felt as though I had been under water for years and had suddenly popped my head above the surface and realised that there was a whole new world out there.

Why is this knowledge so important? Because it totally shifts your perspective on the problem! Before I realised that belief in myself and knowledge of where I wanted to be, were so important, I had blamed *external circumstances* for my lack of success. Believe me, I blamed anything and everybody rather than myself. I said things to myself like:

"If only I had been born rich, or someone had left me some money, then I could do so much."

"If only I had chosen a different profession; this job is a dead-end, it's too late for me to retrain."

"Other people get rich, not me. They probably do it illegally anyway; either that or they're lucky."

"I don't have any special talents or abilities. It's all very well if you're a brilliant designer or a financial whiz, but how will the likes of me get rich?"

And on and on and on! I spent a great deal of time and energy re-enforcing my Negative Self Image, then finding reasons why I could not possibly make a success of my life. I spent many hours doing this; I worked at it very hard!

Are you as guilty as I was? Do you spend time thinking up detailed and plausible reasons why you *can't* have the things you want?

Worse still, do you *firmly believe* that you are a special case, that your unique circumstances totally exclude you from success and happiness? Are you prone to thinking, "It's all very well for him, but..."?

Together, we will shatter the illusion that your present situation is caused by external influences over which you have no control. Using the techniques explained in this book you will come to know for yourself that you can control your own destiny, that you can 'call the shots', that you are not a puppet whose strings are being pulled by some external agency.

It is because *belief in yourself* and *knowledge of where you want to be* are so vitally important to success, that this book is devoted totally to convincing you of these facts.

I am not going to try and tell you exactly *how* to achieve your goals in practical terms, although I do give some guidance in a later chapter. I am not going to give you any secret racing formula or lottery system. The reason for this is simple – everyone's goals will be different.

Some of you reading this book will want a million pounds, some will want less, or more. Others reading the book will not want money at all, but perhaps a change of career to a more useful field of employment, or success in their creative endeavours. Obviously no single practical method could cover all of these goals; it would be pointless trying to devise one.

However, it doesn't matter! I would not even have begun to devise the Midas Method if I thought that the secret of success lay in some practical method (like a lottery system or 'Get Rich Quick' scheme). I *know,* (and I hope to convince you), that most of the secret of success is about believing in yourself, and only a *small part* is in actually doing the things needed to bring success.

When you *know* where you are going, and *believe* that you can get there, the results are almost magical! I can't explain it rationally; the path just opens up for you. Things 'just happen'. A desire which was just a 'pipe dream' suddenly becomes a reality.

That is what makes the Midas Method so exciting. By applying yourself to changing your belief structure, the whole world opens up to you!

Right now, I don't expect you to believe that what I say is true, but I do ask you to keep an open mind and not dismiss it out of hand. The only thing which is preventing you – right now – from starting out on the pathway towards success and happiness, is your scepticism. Your rational mind will tell you that it can't possibly be that simple, there must be a catch!

I'm telling you that it REALLY IS SIMPLE! When I suspended my disbelief, eight years ago, I gave myself a chance in life; after all, I had nothing to lose. But what have *you* got to lose? Nothing! If what I am telling you is untrue, then ask yourself why I bothered to write this book at all? It isn't to make money out of writing books, because firstly there's no money in it, (unless you are a top-selling novelist) and secondly I am offering to give you your money back if my system doesn't work!

You will need belief in order to change your life as from today. Belief that I have no ulterior motive in telling you the things which you will read in this book, and most importantly, belief enough to TRY my system. Ultimately, that's all I ask.

Together, let's have a look at BELIEF. The amazing factor which accounts for a massive FIFTY PERCENT of the pathway to success.

BELIEVE IN YOURSELF
YOU'RE WORTH IT!

3

Belief is the first and most important secret of happiness and success.

How much do you believe in yourself? How much do you think that other people or circumstances control your life?

Right now, at this very moment, you are reading this sentence at a certain stage in your life. Think about your life for a minute or two.

Think about the financial side, for a start. How well off are you? Take a look around you at your possessions; think about your bank balance and savings account (if you have either), think about your total wealth.

Now do a little exercise: On a piece of paper, add up your total wealth, (this can be done in a very short period of time). Do it roughly; there's no need to be exact. Write down your big assets first, with an approximate price next to them, then your most expensive possessions, then the approximate value of your other possessions.

The result could look something like this:

```
House (less mortgage owing).....................25,000
Car............................................ 1,000
Total savings ................................. 2,500
T.V. .......................................... 200
Video.......................................... 300
Jewellery ..................................... 1,000
Household equipment (cooker etc)............... 2,000
HI-FI ......................................... 200
Other household items.......................... 3,000
All furniture ................................. 5,000
Clothes........................................ 2,500

TOTAL ........................................ 42,700
```

You may think that the person in the above example is rich, or poor, depending upon your own circumstances. That doesn't matter; just write down your own figures and add them up.

Please don't skip this exercise or any of the others which I suggest; they are a vital part of your training. I know the temptation is just to carry on reading; but fight it! Take time out to do the exercises; they will pay big dividends.

Now look at your total. How do you *feel* about your total financial worth? Are you happy or unhappy about it at this stage of your life? The chances are that you would like to do better; probably a lot better.

Now I want you to try something: Imagine being in a better financial position. Strongly visualise yourself driving the car you *really want* or living in the house you have always desired; spend a little time over this until you can really imagine yourself in this better position.

Now ask yourself a vital question:- "Do I believe that I am *worth* this?" Ask yourself this question now. Think about it for as long as it takes to come up with an answer; (and that can be a surprisingly long time for such a simple question).

Think about the house or the room(s) where you live. The chances are that you want a better place to live – I have never met anyone who didn't – so think about the next step up for you.

If you live in one room, imagine your own self-contained flat.

If you live in a flat, or a semi, imagine that you are in your own detached house.

If you live in a detached house, think about a larger one with more rooms in a more exclusive area. Hold the image in your mind and ask yourself, "Am I worth it? Do I deserve this?"

Don't be distracted by practical considerations of *how* you might achieve this step forward, just ask yourself if you believe that you *deserve* it.

If the answer is an emphatic "YES!" then great; you are well on your way to achieving more. If the answer comes back as "NO" or you are unsure, then join the club of millions of people who have not yet started to believe in themselves. Right now you are totally trapped by your lack of belief. No wonder you don't have the things you want – like a nicer place to live. You don't believe that you are worth it!

Until you start believing in your own worth, there is not a single chance in ten thousand that you will ever achieve the happiness you really deserve. Why? Because no matter how hard your conscious self works towards achieving these things, your subconscious *knows* that you are not worth it! Your subconscious will go to great lengths to sabotage all your efforts and ensure failure – your conscious and subconscious minds will not be working as a team!

In fact they will be pulling in opposite directions, like a tug of war. Unlike most tug of wars, where the teams are evenly balanced, in this case the odds are highly uneven because the subconscious ALWAYS WINS...unless you use the correct method – the Midas Method – to add a little extra muscle!

What will happen if your conscious mind is trying to improve your lot in life, but your subconscious mind is working, like an underground resistance organisation, to foil your plans?

I'll tell you. Your best laid plans and efforts will 'accidentally' come to grief. You will make silly mistakes which will ensure failure. You will have a terrible run of 'bad luck', or maybe sudden ill-health will prevent you from attending a vital meeting, or going on holiday, or something else which is important to you.

In short, your subconscious mind will try every trick going to ensure that your efforts are neutralised. And it WILL win. Your conscious mind knows nothing at all about these secret plans of sabotage and mayhem! It thinks that it is trying *really hard* to achieve the things it wants. It *can't understand* why things keep going wrong. It is *amazed* that every time it gets close to achieving a major goal, something always seems to go wrong at the last minute!

After trying for a few times and failing, the conscious mind will start calling "FOUL!" and begin blaming external agencies for its downfall. You will start complaining about "bad luck" and "everyone being against you"; eventually you will reach the rational conclusion that there is no point in trying any more!

Then you will give up.

In fact the conscious mind was right. A foul *was* being committed, but it came from a member of its own team! Instead of looking *outside* for the offender, the conscious mind should have been looking *inside* !

Handsomely Equipped to Fail

I know a man who, outwardly, is a very successful businessman and a brilliant salesman. I worked with this man for many years and I always admired his enthusiasm and dedication to his business. He worked really hard – sometimes twelve hours a day and most weekends. This man was going places.

Outwardly he appeared to believe in himself and what he was doing. He knew that he wanted to be a millionaire and to run a large, successful company; and he knew how to get there.

I'll be honest with you and tell you that I wanted to be like this man; he seemed so sure of himself and where he was going.

I'm only glad now that I didn't follow too closely in his footsteps!

The first disaster came after I had known him for only a year. His business suffered a terrible setback and nearly went bust, resulting in him having to work even harder in order to save the company. I felt really sorry for his 'bad luck', but also somewhat puzzled about how the disaster could have happened in the first place. It seemed to me that he had made a number of fundamental business mistakes.

Then other 'accidents' started to happen. Some time after he had saved the business, things started to look really good for him. His enthusiasm increased and he redoubled his efforts to make a success of it. All the ingredients were there and the business started to take off.

But whoops! Disaster struck again, and knocked him back down to a level lower than he had initially started from.

This cycle happened at least five times, and it became obvious to me that this was not a coincidence! No-one could have so much bad luck; it had to be sabotage! I watched the man carefully during all of this, and began to notice how he was subconsciously sabotaging himself to ensure failure.

That's right! He was ensuring his own failure! Why? Because although consciously he was *trying really hard* for success, subconsciously he didn't believe that he was worth it, and so consequently his subconscious took the necessary steps to ensure that he failed! This man did not have a Positive Self Image.

I watched him trying to sell a large order, at boardroom level, to a major

Corporation; he was brilliant. The people liked him, they liked his company and his product; they were ready to sign an order worth tens of thousands of pounds. All he needed to do was to shut up!

Instead, to my horror, he carried on selling! He started inventing wilder and wilder reasons why they should give him the business, (they were ready to anyway). He went on and on and on...

At first, the gathered executives started to look bored, then incredulous. One or two even suppressed a laugh. In short, he had blown the deal and turned a certain order into a disaster. Furthermore, he could not seem to understand what he had done wrong!

At another sales-pitch, I watched him sell over one hundred thousand pound's worth of equipment to a major U.K. company. This equipment was to be distributed to every office of the company and would help them to increase sales. Again, he had closed the deal and they were ready to sign, but at this point he introduced his 'master plan' which, he explained to the assembled buyers, was one further reason why they should buy from him.

His 'master plan' consisted of a method of servicing the equipment, (located all over the country), at a low cost to the client.

His proposal? To use senior citizens to do the servicing, because, he explained, they had plenty of spare time and could make use of cheap rail concessions to travel to service calls at half price!

The assembled audience went very quiet, waiting for the punch-line – which never came. It gradually dawned on them that he was serious, and a few embarrassed coughs signaled the loss of another large order.

I haven't seen this man for several years, but the last I heard he had lost his house and practically everything he owned. To this day, I'm sure that he still has no idea at all why he failed.

He's probably starting another company right now, and hoping that he has better 'luck'.

Digging Holes

I have told you about this man in some detail because I want you to understand that it is not enough just to *say* that you believe in yourself; you must *really* believe in yourself.

It is not enough to work really hard towards your goals. As you have seen from my story, hard work brought my friend nothing but disaster.

To give a silly example:- You could work hard all week long digging a large hole in the ground, then work hard all the following week filling it in again! You would have put two weeks of solid effort into something and achieved nothing!

Most people spend a lot of their lives digging holes and filling them in again.

As I said right at the beginning of this chapter, the actual *work* associated with achieving your goals represents only twenty five percent of the task. Believing in yourself, believing that you are worth it, represents over 50% of the task. That is why I am dwelling on this important subject. If you do not truly believe that you are worth it, all your hard work will come to nothing. You will be like my friend, working hard, day after day, trying, striving and sweating towards your goals, when all along, your subconscious mind is assuring your failure.

IF YOU DON'T BELIEVE IN YOURSELF YOU ARE HANDSOMELY EQUIPPED TO FAIL!

No amount of effort on your part will assure your success. Not even luck will work. If your Great-Aunt Aggie left you a fortune, and yet you didn't believe that you were worth leaving it to, then within a short while it would be gone, slipping away through your fingers, frittered away on useless schemes and ideas.

Two Types of Belief

I have talked a little bit about one type of belief, the belief in your fundamental worth as a human being, the belief that you *deserve* all the things you are striving for. This type of belief stems from having a Positive Self Image.

I have called this type of belief PSI-belief, (Positive Self Image Belief). It is the single most important factor in achieving success and MUST be obtained before you can succeed.

Later, I'll show you how to increase your PSI-belief to a point where you can achieve all of your dreams and ambitions.

The other type of belief is your belief in your ABILITY to achieve your goals. This type of belief is easier to get than PSI-belief, but it is an equally important ingredient of your success equation.

I call this belief I-CAN belief.

Both PSI and I-CAN are ESSENTIAL before you can succeed.

Both of these beliefs must be in place before you can start seriously working towards your major life-goals.

PSI BELIEF IS BELIEF IN YOURSELF.

I-CAN BELIEF IS BELIEF IN YOUR ABILITIES.

These two beliefs are quite distinct and separate from one another. The first is much more important than the second, and far harder to obtain; but I repeat that BOTH must be obtained before you can succeed.

My friend in the story was lacking in PSI-belief but he did have I-CAN belief. His lack of PSI meant that he did not believe that he *deserved* to succeed; he didn't think that he was *worth* it. I-CAN is your belief in your ability to achieve something. Whilst it rests upon the foundation of PSI it is a more intellectual and rational belief.

Interestingly enough, my friend was not lacking in this second type of belief;

he genuinely, (and correctly), believed in his sales ability. But he was severely lacking in PSI-belief, so whilst he knew what he wanted, and believed in his ability to get it, he didn't believe that he was *worth* it – so he failed.

Because this is such an important point, I want to summarise what I have just said:

PSI-belief is concerned with how you *feel* inside about yourself. It is about having a Positive Self Image; knowing that you deserve more, that you are worth it.

I-CAN belief is concerned with convincing yourself that you are ABLE to achieve your goals.

I want you to clearly understand the difference between these two types of belief, so let me give you an example which will help you:

Mary, David and Sue have always longed to go on a skiing holiday. Mary is lacking in both PSI and I-CAN belief. Let's hear what she has to say:

MARY: "I would love to go on a skiing holiday but I have so much to do at home, there's the dog to feed as well, and it would be selfish of me to take a break whilst the children are so young. Anyway, I'm really clumsy; I'd never get the hang of it."

TRANSLATION: "My needs are less important than a dog's and I couldn't do it anyway."

David is lacking in PSI-belief: Let's listen to him:

DAVID: "Skiing is for rich people, not for the likes of us. Pity really because I'm sure I would be good at it."

TRANSLATION: "I'm a second-class citizen and I'm going to make sure that I stay that way. I don't doubt my abilities though."

Sue is lacking in I-CAN belief. Here's what she might say:

SUE: "A holiday is a really great idea. I deserve a break after the year I've just had. The children can go to my Mother's, she'd love to have them and the change would do them good. Does it have to be skiing though? You have to be really athletic and muscular don't you?"

TRANSLATION: "I feel good about myself inside and know that I am worth this break. However, I have doubts about my abilities, and I'm a bit scared of this unknown challenge."

These examples should help you to understand how different the two beliefs are.

I am now going to tell you something which you might find surprising:

PSI-belief is to do with FEELINGS and EMOTIONS about yourself, and is not easily improved by logical argument, whereas I-CAN belief is more rational, and is open to logical argument.

This becomes obvious when we look at our skiing friends.

No amount of rational, logical argument about how easy it is to ski, how cheap the kennels are, or how much the children might enjoy her being away, will convince MARY to go on this holiday. Why? Because she doesn't think she is worth it! All this talk of dogs and children is just a smoke-screen to give her an excuse for not going.

If I *did* try to convince her, the conversation would go something like this:

ME: "Mary, why don't you take this break, you deserve it!"

MARY: "But who would look after the dog?"

ME: "There are plenty of excellent kennels close by, but if you don't fancy them then I could look after it for you."

MARY: "Thanks; but it's not just the dog. Don't forget I'm a Mother and have certain *responsibilities* to my children. I can't just get up and leave them."

ME: "Sure you can! They're old enough now, and you've told me many times that your Mother would love to have them."

MARY: "That's true, but I couldn't really *afford* to go. There are so many other things I should spend my money on, like clothes for the children."

ME: "Why not spend it on yourself just this once?"

MARY: "Anyway, I couldn't leave the house empty for all that time, there are lots of burglaries around here."

And on and on and on! One excuse after another. Do you see what I mean? Mary's practical problems are purely incidental to the central message which runs through her every sentence. This message is: "I'm not worth it. I should spend money on other people not me. I don't deserve a holiday."

Do you see that no amount of rational talking or explanation can help Mary?

SUE, however, is a different proposition. She has a fundamentally Positive Self Image; all she needs is a little convincing and reassurance. I could probably persuade her to go if I told her about the easy slopes, the beginner's classes, and the fact that there would be dozens of people just like her. In other words, by presenting a rational argument, I stand a good chance of boosting Sue's I-CAN belief.

A talk with Sue might go something like this:

SUE: "I've never been skiing before, I couldn't do it. Surely you have to be really fit?"

ME: "Nonsense! Most of the people going won't have skied before. There are beginner's classes and excellent training."

SUE: "I'm too old though. They're all youngsters aren't they?"

ME: "Are you joking? Last time I went there were three people over sixty who were there for the first time!"

SUE: "I'd be scared of hurtling down those long slopes like you see on the television."

ME: (Laughing), "You only get to go on those slopes when you're good and ready. You'll be starting out on the flat!"

SUE: "Really? Perhaps it would be fun after all."

A little more rational argument and Sue might be willing to go.
Notice the difference between Mary's message and Sue's message:

MARY IS SAYING:- "I'm not worth it."

SUE IS SAYING:- "I can't do that."

These are very different statements.
Notice also, how I was able to persuade Sue by rational argument? A lot of the actual text of this book is designed to do just that; increase your belief in your abilities (I-CAN) by presenting you with a reasoned argument.

Increasing your belief in your own worth (PSI), is a far more difficult proposition, because, as I have said, it is not amenable to rational argument. No amount of reasonable, logical argument on my part will increase your feeling of self-worth by one jot.

But because it is VITAL that you have a Positive Self Image, a large part of the method is devoted to increasing your belief in your self-worth.

Do you remember at the start of this chapter I asked you to take a little time over asking yourself the question, "Do I deserve a larger house?" This is because I knew that PSI-belief was not easily approached by such intellectual questions. PSI belief is lodged so firmly in the subconscious mind, that I asked you to IMAGINE being in your new home.

The coins of the subconscious mind are IMAGES, just as the coins of the conscious or rational mind are THOUGHTS.

How Do I Know If I Have a Negative Self Image?

If, like my friend, you have a Negative Self Image which is impeding your progress, then it MUST be corrected before you have any chance at all of succeeding.

Correcting this NSI represents the fundamental foundation of the Midas

Method. Without it you are wasting your time trying to achieve any of your life-goals. With a nasty NSI lurking in your subconscious, your very best efforts are doomed to failure.

I will show you how to eradicate this NSI later in the book, after you have completed an interesting quiz which determines the level of your NSI; but it is important that you realise the difference between PSI-belief and I-CAN belief at this stage.

The actual level of your PSI-belief will determine the amount of time you have to spend improving it. All readers will have to spend SOME time on this vital area.

Because all this talk about conscious and subconscious minds can be confusing, let me summarise this chapter briefly:

YOU WILL NOT ACHIEVE YOUR GOALS WITHOUT BELIEF.

THERE ARE TWO TYPES OF BELIEF:- PSI BELIEF AND I-CAN BELIEF.

PSI-Belief reflects how you FEEL about yourself deep down inside.

It is about your level of self-worth. PSI-belief CANNOT be improved by rational argument, reading books, or discussion. It CAN be improved by the type of exercise given later in this book. You MUST have a Positive Self Image if you are to succeed – you must believe that YOU ARE WORTH all the good things in life, you must believe that YOU DESERVE IT. Without this belief you will fail.

I-CAN belief reflects how capable you think you are on a 'nuts and bolts' level. It concerns how you THINK about your abilities and what you BELIEVE is possible or not possible for you. It is largely a learned response and is heavily determined by your upbringing and schooling.

An example of this is the message: "Women don't become engineers," which effectively prevents all but the most determined women from taking up this profession.

When you have PSI-belief and I-CAN belief then you are HALF WAY to success. YES; HALF WAY!

This is the most difficult and challenging part of the method which I am sharing with you.

Formula of Success

We are now in a position to re-write our simple formula for success given at the start of the book:

SUCCESS IS:

25% PSI-BELIEF.
25% I-CAN BELIEF.
25% KNOWING WHAT YOU WANT.
25% GETTING THERE.

Well, PSI and I-CAN added together make a giant 50% of the formula!

You are now well on your way to understanding why belief is so important to your success. Let us now examine PSI-belief in detail, and see how we can improve it.

PSI-BELIEF

4

PSI (pronounced "sigh"), means Positive Self Image. We should all have a Positive Self Image if we are to be happy, successful, loving and complete human beings. Unfortunately, few of us have a very strong PSI, and a lot of us have a pronounced Negative Self Image (NSI).

In the previous chapter I told you how lack of PSI-belief WILL prevent you from achieving the things you want in life. How much it will prevent you, depends entirely upon the depth of your Negative Self Image.

There is a very simple relationship between your PSI and your achievement potential:- The STRONGER your PSI, the MORE you will achieve.

The converse is also true:- The STRONGER your NSI, the LESS you will achieve.

Remember that this is INDEPENDENT of your abilities, and independent of 'luck', although these two are frequently blamed for the failure which always accompanies a Negative Self Image.

I also told you that PSI cannot be improved by rational argument, this is because the subconscious mind does not understand argument, and PSI is buried deep in the subconscious.

Therefore I will not devote this chapter to telling you what a really wonderful human being you are and how you deserve all the things you really want in life. Although this is true, it will not have much of an effect on your Negative Self Image. Instead I want to explain a little bit about how people get Negative Self Images in the first place; then I'll tell you how to dramatically improve your PSI to the point where you can unlock the doorway to success.

Where Does NSI Come From?

All people are dealt a full hand of PSI at birth.

Deep in the womb, the baby feels warm, relaxed and safe. It has no inkling of the potential dangers which lie outside. If it could enter into a discussion with you, it would probably say that it felt valued and wanted; in other words, it would have a high PSI-level. (Arguments about pre-birth traumas aside for the moment.)

After birth, the baby enters the 'stage of life' upon which will be enacted an important drama. All good drama has conflict as an underlying theme; and in this case the conflict is between the forces which increase the child's PSI level, and those which decrease it.

You entered onto this stage the moment you were born, and since that moment, you have been subjected to some forces which made you feel good (increased your PSI), and some forces which made you feel bad (decreased your PSI or increased your NSI).

These forces we will call "strokes". (A term borrowed from Dr Eric Berne M.D.)

The present level of your PSI-belief is a direct result of these conflicting strokes throughout your past life.

If you have a high PSI, then you received more (or better quality) positive strokes than negative.

If you have a low PSI, then you received more (or stronger) negative strokes than positive.

I will now tell you something which is very important:

These strokes have far more effect upon your PSI when you are younger than when you are older. (By 'older' I mean over about twelve!) Remember also that strokes are stored away subconsciously, so you don't have much access to them via your conscious mind.

Positive and negative strokes started to accumulate when you were born (some would argue before). As a baby you immediately started to store away feelings about your own self-worth (PSI belief), depending upon how your parents handled you and spoke to you. If they spoke softly and were kind, loving and gentle, then your PSI started to increase. On the other hand, if they were rough and unkind, your PSI started to decrease.

In the real world, most babies are neither loved absolutely, or continually brutalised, so you probably received a mixture of positive and negative strokes. Hopefully you received far more positive than negative, but if it was the other way round, then you were off to a bad start with a pronounced NSI.

The process did not stop there. As you grew up into a toddler and learnt to speak, you started to be bombarded with messages intended to alter your PSI one way or another.

Wait a minute! Surely the PSI is not affected by messages like these?

That's right! It is not really affected by the CONTENT of the message (although the I-CAN is!), but it IS affected by the EMOTIONAL TONE of the message. Put simply, the WORDS are not important, it is the WAY THEY ARE SAID which affects your PSI.

For example, you could say really softly, gently and lovingly to a one-year-old: "I wish you would go and boil your head, I can't stand the sight of you!" The chances are that the child would smile sweetly back at you.

Alternatively, you could yell loudly and angrily at the same child: "I think a banana is a yellow skinned fruit!" and no doubt it would burst into tears and become very upset.

The CONTENT was unimportant, it was the EMOTIONAL TONE which had the effect.

I will now tell you something surprising:- **Even when you are old enough to understand language it is STILL the emotional tone of the message which affects your PSI-level and not the content.** (The CONTENT affects your I-CAN level but we will be discussing that in the next chapter.)

Let me give you some examples:-

Danny is four years old and very pleased with the model boat he has just made. He toddles up to Daddy and proudly displays his handiwork.

Daddy says in a flat monotone without looking up from his paper:- "That's really very good Danny, well done." Danny feels dejected and toddles off to play by himself.

Although the CONTENT was correct, the EMOTIONAL TONE did not support it! The EMOTIONAL TONE effectively said: "I don't care about you, I'm far more interested in my newspaper." And this was the message received and filed away in Danny's subconscious.

Score minus-one for Danny's PSI-belief!

How about this though?:- Danny toddles up with his model boat and shows it to Dad. Dad puts down the paper, takes the boat, admires it, smiles broadly at Danny then gives him a great big hug. ALL WITHOUT SAYING A WORD!

Danny goes away glowing with pride, even though the verbal CONTENT of the exchange was zero!

Score plus-one for Danny's PSI-belief!

The messages received between birth and about five years old play a major part in determining your present level of PSI belief. I would estimate that these messages formulated over half of your PSI-belief, and that the remainder came as a result of all the years since!

If at least half of your PSI-belief was formed before you were five, is it any wonder that you cannot access it via your conscious mind? It is there nevertheless and it controls your life as effectively as a puppet-master controls a puppet.

School Days

When you went to school you opened yourself up to an absolute barrage of messages, a great many of these messages affected your PSI-belief.

Even here though, the CONTENT did not really affect your PSI-belief, but the EMOTIONAL TONE certainly did.

Supposing your mathematics mistress took you to one side and said to you very kindly: "Although you have a lively and inquiring mind, and despite the fact that you have tried really hard this year, I feel that maths is probably not the subject for you. However, your many other abilities outweigh this and I have suggested to the headmistress that you be allowed to join the fourth year Latin class."

The CONTENT of this message is a bit of a downer. She is effectively saying that you are useless at maths, AND THIS WILL BE NOTED WELL BY THE I-CAN. However, she has not really affected your feeling of self-worth because her EMOTIONAL TONE suggested that she liked you, and that you were a really worthwhile person.

Contrast this with the treatment your friend receives at the hand of the dreaded Mr Masters: "Pay attention Jones, you disgusting, sniveling little creep! Just because you're top of the class and get every answer right, doesn't give a smart-ass like you permission to dream your worthless life away staring through the window!"

A little extreme perhaps, but the CONTENT was effectively telling Jones that he was really good at maths! (AND THIS WILL BE NOTED BY HIS I-CAN), however, how do you think the message affected his PSI? BADLY! His PSI-belief only heard the EMOTIONAL TONE of the exchange, which effectively told Jones that he was not a worthwhile person, and that the master despised and loathed him.

His PSI-belief will be greatly reduced if exposed to too much of this type of treatment – particularly if it is being strongly re-enforced in his home life.

Out Of School

As we grow up and mature, we become somewhat less sensitive to direct assaults on our PSI-belief. (As I said earlier, a large part of your PSI-belief is formed before the age of five.)

For example, if you were involved in a car accident and an offended party started waving his fists and saying things like: "Your sort shouldn't be allowed on the road", it is unlikely that you would allow this to affect your PSI-level. You would (hopefully) be mature enough to make allowances for circumstances – i.e. that he was upset.

However, a great deal of PSI-damage can be done by a process called 'discounting'. Put simply, anything which discounts you as a human being is likely to decrease your PSI-level. Two trivial examples will suffice – I'm sure we have all experienced these, or something like them:-

You are waiting to get served at a crowded bar. Your turn comes and goes, but no matter what you do the barman seems to ignore you, (although he serves several people on either side of you).

You feel discounted and worthless because the implied message is: "All these people are more important than you, you're worthless."

Or:-You are waiting in a queue, (a peculiarly British pastime), when someone pushes in front of you. Again you feel very upset; not because you have to wait a little longer but because you received the message: "You're so worthless I'm not even going to acknowledge your presence."

Too many of these situations without the compensating positive strokes can cause a gradual decrease in an otherwise mature person's PSI-level.

It is very important that you understand that PSI is a dynamic, changing thing and is affected by daily positive and negative strokes. EVEN THE MOST RUGGED PSI WOULD CRUMBLE IF DEPRIVED OF POSITIVE STROKES FOR TOO LONG.

No person is an island unto themselves. For example, if someone with a really high PSI were to find themselves in solitary confinement, say in a prison camp where they were being continually brutalised, and without access to positive strokes (e.g. other prisoners), it would be an alarmingly short time before their PSI-level was reduced to nothing. This extreme example should serve as a reminder to us that we have to continually maintain our PSI-belief.

Later in the book I'll be giving you methods for improving and maintaining your PSI-level on a daily basis.

I was very excited when I first realised that PSI-belief was VITAL to achieving success, because up until that point I had blamed *external* forces for my lack of achievement. Of course these external forces (lack of money, bad luck etc.) being *external* were OUT OF MY CONTROL. If they were out of my control I couldn't do anything about improving my situation could I? I wasn't to blame! I could happily carry on moaning about my bad fortune, complaining about my lack of abilities, talents or money and starting every other sentence with "If only....". After all, what could I do about it?

When I realised that PSI-belief was the real controlling factor, and that all the other things which I had blamed were MINOR by comparison to this, it was as though I had suddenly woken up. The shock of realisation was quite a powerful and liberating experience. It is my sincere hope that through this book, you will come to have this experience for yourself.

I was still puzzled by one thing though. WHY does your subconscious mind prevent you from achieving all the good things which you deserve? It seemed to me to be plainly stupid that a part of your mind could plot against you to stop you from being happy! I could understand it if it were the other way round, for example if the subconscious mind prevented you from smoking, drinking or taking drugs because it knew that these things would harm you! But the very *reverse* is true. Most of us do some or all of these things KNOWING that they WILL harm us!

The Pay-off

The mind does not do things without a reason. There has to be a 'pay-off' for all behaviour, EVEN NEGATIVE BEHAVIOUR.

The 'pay-off' for *positive* behaviour was obvious to me. We indulge ourselves in good food and drink and we wear nice clothes, because these things feel good and have very few negative effects.

I could also understand the 'pay-off' for physically harmful things like smoking. Obviously the instant pleasure was a stronger influence than the spectre of some possible future health problem.

What I could not understand, for a long time, was WHY the subconscious should seek to prevent you from achieving something good which had no (obvious) negative effects. Why should your lack of PSI make you act in a way which was guaranteed to make you fail, hence make you feel less miserable and worthless and thereby RE-ENFORCE your NSI? It seemed like a vicious circle with no obvious reason or 'pay-off'.

I pondered over this for a long time without coming to a firm conclusion. It seemed to me to be an essential flaw in the argument, an irritating 'missing link'.

A behavioural psychologist could easily have answered my question for me, but at the time I didn't realise this. I had to read several psychology books before I found the answer.

The answer I found in those books may surprise you; it certainly amazed me!

Put very simply, I believe the answer to be this:- The subconscious mind doesn't really care a fig for 'happiness' as such. Happiness is an extremely abstract concept anyway.

A Zen monk is exceedingly happy sitting for long hours every day meditating, whereas you or I might be extremely unhappy doing this.

I might be happy running a large company, whereas this same situation could cause another person extreme distress.

You might be happy painting pictures all day long, but I might find the same thing tedious in the extreme.

I might think that I would be happy with a million pounds, but find that I was unhappy when I actually got it.

The subconscious mind COULDN'T CARE LESS about your goals, ambitions and dreams. It is REALLY NOT INTERESTED in your plans to become a millionaire or your ambitions to run your own chain of designer clothes shops. All these things are as illusory to the subconscious mind as your dreams are to your conscious mind!

The subconscious mind views the conscious mind as a whirlpool of thoughts, ambitions, hopes, half-formed ideas and sensory data and DOESN'T PAY MUCH ATTENTION to the detail – it finds it confusing.

Similarly, the conscious mind views the subconscious mind as a whirlpool of images, feelings emotions and dreams.

I was now on the trail of something big. If the subconscious mind doesn't give a damn about your 'success' or 'lack of success', (two extremely difficult concepts for the subconscious mind to grasp anyway), what *does* it care about?

Physical World View

The answer is SURVIVAL. Or, more accurately, MAINTENANCE OF A COHERENT WORLD VIEW. That's a bit of a mouthful, but what it really means is that the subconscious is DESPERATELY trying to make sense of the external world and your place in it.

Furthermore, IT DOESN'T LIKE CHANGING ITS BELIEF IN THE WAY THE WORLD IS! No sir, not one little bit! It doesn't mind making the odd little adjustment to the picture; a little tweak here and there to keep the picture in line with the facts, but it HATES making any major changes.

Why is this?

Because the WORLD VIEW, which you painstakingly pieced together in your very early years, is an essential survival tool. Without a consistent World View you are doomed.

Your World View tells you that a floor in a room is likely to support you as you walk across it. It tells you that most people are friendly and are unlikely to suddenly attack you unprovoked. It tells you that rain will not kill you but that electricity might. It tells you that you can drink water but not bleach.

If you had to work these things out for yourself every time you encountered them, you could not possibly survive. It's hard enough surviving your *first* electric shock or brush with fire!

The Mental Jigsaw

There are thousands upon thousands of pieces to this jigsaw puzzle which the subconscious mind painstakingly put together, through bitter and painful experience, to comprise a picture of the world and how you fit into it. It was hard-won!

Because this picture is so hard-won and required real EFFORT to construct, the subconscious mind is VERY RELUCTANT to change large, firmly established pieces of the main puzzle.

Unlike real jigsaw puzzles, the WORLD VIEW picture is growing all the time as you find out new things about the world around you, but at your age, these are changes to the periphery of the puzzle and are quite minor; they do not affect the main body of the picture.

For example, you might watch a T.V. documentary on fashion trends in the young and thereby expand your World View to include the possibility that short skirts were back in fashion. But if another T.V. documentary told you that the moon was made of cheese, you would strongly suspect a spoof!

The first example involved a change only to the periphery of your World View jigsaw, so you were willing to accept it, but the second example threatened a change to some of your central pieces, so your subconscious mind rejected it.

But the moon really *could* be made of cheese for all you know! You've never been there or touched it, so how do you know? Obviously the *facts* don't matter so much to the subconscious, it is *belief* which holds those central pieces of the puzzle firmly in place.

This is why people who hold deep-seated irrational beliefs like racial prejudices, do not require the inconvenience of facts to back them up; belief is quite enough.

Changing the Puzzle

What happens if you try to change one of the main pieces of the puzzle?

The answer is that the subconscious mind will respond strongly with FEAR and RESISTANCE to the change. It will ask the conscious mind to examine the data again and again to see if the change is real, or whether it can be squeezed into the existing World View.

It will effectively ask: "ARE YOU REALLY SURE ABOUT THIS???"

If the change is a really big one then a mental breakdown could result, such is the strength of the subconscious resistance to changes in the main body of the picture!

For example: Supposing you walked into a room and saw a man suddenly rise up from the floor and hover, suspended in mid-air, six inches from the ceiling. This event would seriously undermine a major piece of your World View puzzle. (The piece which says that people cannot defy gravity without artificial means.)

Your first response would be SHOCK. Shock at such a basic piece of the jigsaw being violated. The conscious mind would attempt to change the World View of the subconscious mind by saying: "Look, a flying man!" The subconscious mind would respond with, "NO WAY!"

Such would be the reluctance of the subconscious mind to change the World View, that it would INSIST upon the conscious mind examining the facts very carefully again.

So you would dutifully examine every detail of the floating man. You would check carefully for ropes or wires, mirrors or other foul means of deception. Then you would pass this summarised data back to the subconscious mind; effectively saying, "Sorry, but it really *is* a floating man!"

The subconscious mind would STILL REFUSE TO ACCEPT THIS, and certainly would NOT start to alter the basic World View. It would suggest that the conscious mind look yet again! It must be a joke, surely? Or a trick; yes, someone was playing a trick! It wasn't a real man up there, probably a hydrogen-filled balloon in the shape of a man.

In short, the subconscious would try ANYTHING, no matter how wild, to convince itself that what was being experienced could be fitted into the EXISTING World View. It would FIGHT and SCREAM and KICK against making any alterations to that World View.

If, despite everything, the conscious mind could find no trickery, deception or illusion; would the subconscious then grudgingly accept that men could, under certain circumstances, float up to the ceiling? NO WAY! NOT A CHANCE! Instead, you would run out of the room screaming with terror! Anything rather than change such a basically-held belief.

Later on, you would go over the incident and think up some logical explanation for the event; something you had missed at the time, some reasonable method which would account for what you had seen. It was probably a publicity stunt; the man MUST have been supported somehow, after all, it was no different to those conjurors on the television, they were always doing things like that weren't they?

When your subconscious mind had seized upon an explanation, no matter how bizarre, it would breathe a BIG SIGH OF RELIEF at not having to change the World View! Everything would be back to normal, it could relax.

The Mystery Horse

Here is something which happened to me recently:-

One night I walked into my bedroom without bothering to switch on the light. I nearly died with fright! There, lurking in the corner, was the shadow of a giant horse!

My World View was being hit hard! How could a horse be in my bedroom? It wasn't possible! My subconscious mind didn't believe it either, and asked me to look again. Closer examination revealed, not a horse but a crane. A crane? That was just as daft! The subconscious again refused to start tinkering with the jigsaw and asked me to check more carefully. I went through several other possibilities in my mind before I realised that it was the new bookshelf which I had installed that very day, casting a strange shadow on the wall.

All this happened in the space of less than one second!

This fascinating experience gave me great insight into how the subconscious mind works. It FEARS changes in the World View and it will desperately try to fit a known explanation onto the unknown event, in an attempt to make it CONSISTENT with its existing World View. It will try every combination of ideas to explain the unknown, until it comes up with one which fits. If, despite trying everything, it is still confronted with the unknown, then it will often PANIC and run a mile! This has great survival value.

Obviously the World View can, and does change. The subconscious is not set in concrete! However, pieces of the jigsaw which are considered inviolate require a great deal of *effort* to change. Other pieces of lesser importance require less effort to change.

Five Wheels on my Wagon

For example, most cars have four wheels. If you saw one which had five wheels you would look at it for some time and try to evaluate it. Eventually you would be prepared to consider the possibility that five-wheeled cars do exist, but this change is unlikely to cause you major problems.

However, it is interesting to note that even such a minor change as this is likely to cause you to comment on it to friends and associates: "Hey, you'll never guess what I saw today....", because the subconscious mind is SEEKING RE-ASSURANCE on even this minor point. It wants other people to say: "Haven't you seen a five-wheeled car before? They're getting *really common* now!" Then it can RELAX and stop worrying about this irritating unknown event.

Let me tell you in four simple sentences how the subconscious mind operates in this instance:

IT BUILDS A CONSISTENT WORLD VIEW (Mainly in the early years)

IT ACCEPTS SMALL ALTERATIONS (But grudgingly)

IT FEARS AND REJECTS LARGE ALTERATIONS

IT TAKES INCREDIBLE EFFORT TO CHANGE LARGE PIECES OF THE JIGSAW

Obviously the subconscious mind is vastly more complex than this, and has been the subject of many books and a great deal of scholarly thought, but this simple explanation will suffice for our purposes.

I have told you a little about how the subconscious mind likes to build a physical picture of the world around it. This is essential if you are to survive. However, in addition to building a nice, cozy picture of the physical world around you, the subconscious mind also likes to build another picture which is equally as powerful.

This is the picture of WHO you are and HOW you fit into the society and environment around you. It it this facet of the World View which is important to our discussions.

Here is something very interesting:

The subconscious mind works in EXACTLY the same way when it comes to defending its views about WHO you are and WHAT you are, as it does to defending its picture of how the outside physical world should behave.

In other words, the subconscious will KICK HARD against any attempt to change your beliefs about *who* and *what* you are.

And the pay-off is............. SECURITY!

To the subconscious mind, SECURITY is everything. It will vigorously oppose any attempt on your part to change the World View, and it will do this DESPITE ANY EFFECT ON YOUR 'HAPPINESS'!!

As I said earlier, it couldn't care less about your happiness, but it DOES care about SECURITY – the security of a consistent World View.

This was the answer to the question which had been puzzling me for so long. Here was the secret of WHY a lack of PSI prevented you from achieving all of the things which you deserved.

The subconscious mind is SCARED of changing main pieces of your social jigsaw just as it is of changing main pieces of your physical jigsaw. Once it has worked out where you fit into the social scale, IT IS MOST RELUCTANT TO MAKE A CHANGE TO THIS PICTURE.

Your earliest experiences affected your PSI-belief until your subconscious mind had built up a nice, solid picture of WHO you were, and HOW MUCH YOU WERE WORTH as an individual. During the first few years of your life, your Positive Self Image (or lack of it), became firmly established in the subconscious mind; it became, (along with many other things), one of the CENTRAL pieces of the jigsaw; remember this, not an OUTSIDE piece (where the jigsaw can grow), but a CENTRAL piece.

This social picture covers many topics, for example it defines:

Your 'Class'.
How you feel about yourself.
How you think others feel about you.
How much you feel you are 'worth'.
How lovable you are.
How much you feel you deserve.

And many, many more things.

All those positive and negative strokes received during your formative years, helped the subconscious to build a firm level of PSI-belief, which was then added to the rest of the social jigsaw to form a nice, cosy World View. Whilst the subconscious mind is happy to tinker around with the *edges* of this picture, it HATES to touch the main body of the picture because of the INSECURITY which this will bring.

That is why the methods which I will share with you are so powerful! When you alter your PSI-belief you swap some pretty large pieces of jigsaw puzzle.

This will cause FEAR and INSECURITY in your subconscious and you must be prepared to deal with these whilst your PSI is being overhauled.

Believe me it is a small price to pay for the lasting happiness and success which my method will bring you.

A Place For Everyone

There is a saying that "Everyone likes to know their place." I have found this to be very true!

Some time ago I went to a party where I did not know many people.

I was apprehensive about this party because I had not been told much about it. For example, I did not know what type of party it would be (e.g. dinner or disco), what dress standards were expected of me, what time to arrive, what to bring, or really anything very much at all.

I guessed at the clothes I should wear, (something nice and safe to cover the maximum number of possibilities), took along a bottle of quite good wine (just good enough for dinner but not too good for a disco), and arrived at a fashionably safe eight o'clock.

I took this opportunity to examine how my subconscious mind was working – and I was really amazed! (You have to be very alert to catch your subconscious mind in operation because it acts very quickly.)

I walked into that room, (clutching my bottle of wine), and my subconscious mind was ALIVE and RACING in an effort to evaluate the social position as rapidly as possible. So DESPERATE was I to work out my social position in this strange group, that for a good ten seconds I just stood in the doorway, soaking up data.

My eyes raced around the room examining a cross-section of the people there; men first, then women. (Had I been a woman it would have been the other way round.) In under two seconds I had scanned twenty people and worked out an average standard of dress, compared it with my own, and filed away the difference. (Not too significant, I was about right.)

My subconscious mind breathed a small sigh of relief!

Then my eyes flitted round the room and evaluated the whole 'scene' as one entity. Within less than a second I had evaluated the 'type of party', and compared it with the complete list of every other party I had ever been to in my life, before filing it away under the heading which fitted best -'Smart disco/buffet'.

Since I had been to many such parties, I also attached an anxiety level to this information – (low anxiety).

My subconscious mind breathed a slightly larger sigh of relief.

IT WAS STILL ONLY THREE SECONDS SINCE I HAD WALKED THROUGH THE DOOR!

I was a bit more relaxed by now, so I took a leisurely two seconds to examine the groupings of people. Since I was on my own, I was looking to see if people were mainly in couples, or if there were quite a few obviously single people.

I could relax again; there were quite a few single people.

After this, I took three seconds to evaluate the average CLASS of the people at the party. This incredible feat involved scanning about thirty people at random and making value-judgments about each one's clothes, hair, posture, face, voice and manner; then averaging the whole lot to arrive at an 'average class' of the party, (chosen from an internal subconscious scale of about 100 sub-classes). I compared this average with my own class (a deeply held PSI-belief), and worked out if I was higher or lower class than most of the people there.

The subconscious mind didn't really care if I was higher OR lower class so long as I was ABOUT THE SAME as most of the people there. What it feared was the UNKNOWN situation of spending an evening with people of a very different class.

I could relax! My subconscious mind was not being forced to re-evaluate its World View. My level of fear diminished and I walked into the room with confidence.

Total elapsed time? Under ten seconds!

In America, and other nearly classless societies, an identical process would be carried out, but with wealth as the criteria rather than class. In Britain, despite what anyone says, it is definitely CLASS which people evaluate first, THEN their comparative wealth.

Do you see how my subconscious mind was DESPERATE to know where it fitted in? It was REALLY SCARED about that party, until it had evaluated the data collected by the conscious mind and worked out exactly where the party fitted into its World View.

Had I walked into that room to find everyone dressed in funny blue uniforms and doing a dance which I had never seen before, I would have been REALLY ANXIOUS, almost to the point of turning and running! I would have spent the first few minutes FRANTICALLY trying to work out where I fitted into this party, and how I related to these people.

An Experiment

Parties are excellent places for realising the extent to which your subconscious needs to know where you fit in.

You can try this interesting experiment for yourself: Next time you are at a party and a stranger asks you what you do, try the following style of conversation:

Stranger: "What do you do?" (They mean for a living.)

You: "Do? Well sometimes I play golf."

Stranger: "Oh! You're a golfer."

You: "No, I just play golf sometimes."

Stranger: "I see, but what do you really do?"

You: "I read quite a lot."

Stranger: "Do you work in a library?"

You: "No, but I like books."

Stranger: "Where do you work?"

You: "At home."

Stranger: "Oh, you're self employed! What do you do?"

You: "Well sometimes I play golf..."

Obviously this is not guaranteed to win you many friends, but the object of the experiment is to avoid giving the other person any concrete information about yourself for as long as possible. Then watch them get more and more upset until they walk away!

Why do they get so upset? It is because their subconscious mind is struggling hard to 'classify' you, to get you neatly pigeon-holed under the heading, 'Writer, lower-upper-middle class, fairly well off, unmarried, fanciable but not sexy,' or whatever particular label applies to you.

Until their subconscious mind can file you away in this manner, it cannot relax because its immediate World View is unknown. Their ANGER stems from FEAR.

So now you know something about PSI-belief! You know that it is ESSENTIAL to have a high level of PSI-belief before you can achieve all the things which you desire. I have told you that your level of PSI-belief is formed very early on in your life as a result of positive and negative strokes which you received.

You also know that this PSI-belief is a *deeply held conviction* on the part of your subconscious; it is a central piece of the main jigsaw puzzle which forms the picture of the world, and the subconscious is VERY RELUCTANT to change it.

In fact rather than change the level of PSI-belief, the subconscious will FORCE you to act in a manner which 'proves' that the currently held level of PSI-belief is correct.

How Does This Work?

Put simply; if your PSI-belief tells you that you are a failure and do not deserve to succeed, your subconscious will make you act in a way which is GUARANTEED to ensure failure, rather than change a piece of the main jigsaw picture. In this way it ensures *stability* and *security*.

Do you remember my business friend? Do you see now why he failed? His subconscious KNEW that he did not *deserve* to succeed, a central piece of his jigsaw had the words "You're useless", written on them. Despite the best efforts of his conscious mind to change his circumstances, his subconscious was NOT WILLING to tinker around with basically-held beliefs. It was far more interested in SECURITY and MAINTAINING ITS WORLD VIEW.

The result? The subconscious forced my friend to act in a way which would ensure failure, thereby PROVING the subconscious right! The subconscious could now relax again because its World View was not being threatened, leaving my poor friend's conscious mind to wonder what went wrong!

In the second section of the book, I'll be showing you how to BOOST your PSI-belief, thereby removing one of the main obstacles in the path of success. Once you have been freed from NSI, the SKY IS THE LIMIT! You can achieve ANYTHING which you want to. You will no longer limit yourself to second best but instead, you will travel FIRST-CLASS through life. Why? Because you will know that you deserve it.

I-CAN BELIEF

5

YES! You CAN achieve ANYTHING that you want!

Well; nearly anything............!

I often say this to people only to have them give silly examples of things which they CANNOT do. For instance they will say: "I really want to fly to the moon by flapping my arms; how can I do that?" or : "I'm seventy-five but I want to become the heavyweight boxing champion of the world!"

I get exasperated at this because obviously there are many things which you cannot do and will never do. Your physical limitations (alone) will put a ceiling on your level of achievement.

I call this *absolute* limit to your potential the REAL CEILING. Your REAL CEILING height is set by things like your age (and hence physical ability), and by what is 'impossible', in the true (rather than imagined) sense of the word.

For the purpose of illustration, I would like you to imagine this REAL CEILING to be like the ceiling of a huge cathedral. Imagine this ceiling to be over ONE HUNDRED feet above you. This represents the REAL ceiling to your achievements.

It may surprise you to know that most people spend their entire lives living and working under a FALSE ceiling. Furthermore, this FALSE ceiling is set much, much lower than the real ceiling, thereby effectively preventing people from achieving things which are readily achievable.

Now then, how high do you think your FALSE ceiling is in comparison to the REAL ceiling? You'll be amazed when I tell you that most people's false ceilings are under *three feet* high. YES; THREE FEET!

Let me say that again:

MOST PEOPLE ARE WORKING UNDER A FALSE CEILING WHICH IS LESS THAN THREE FEET HIGH!

They are crammed into this artificially small space without even room to lift their heads! Do you see why I get annoyed at the silly examples?

People who give examples of silly things which they CANNOT do, are pointing out the limitations of a one hundred foot ceiling, whilst they themselves are working under a three foot ceiling!

It is rather like saying to someone: "Hah! Your Rolls Royce can only go at 130 mph", when all the time you are riding a child's tricycle!

YES, there are things which you cannot and will not achieve; but these things are so far above your present FALSE ceiling that they are irrelevant.

Why worry about not being able to fly to the moon if you haven't even taken a holiday for the last five years?

Why worry about being heavyweight champion of the world if you cannot even give up smoking?

Why worry about being able to buy America if you cannot even pay off your mortgage?

I'll tell you something else:- Although the *real ceiling* to your achievements is one hundred feet high, your *wildest dreams* of wealth, power and happiness are set at around the fifty foot mark; in other words, they are well below the *real* ceiling – they are easily achievable! I'll say that again in case you missed it:- Your wildest dreams of wealth, power and happiness are easily achievable.

The statement at the start of this chapter should say: "You can achieve anything providing it is sensible and within human capabilities." But this doesn't have quite the same ring, does it?

So I say that you can achieve ANYTHING AT ALL, and trust that you are sensible enough to realise the implied human limitation of the one hundred foot ceiling.

Stand Up Straight!

Think of the fantastic feeling of relief that you would experience if you could raise your FALSE CEILING from its present low height to the full one hundred foot height! It would be like being born again! You could do ANYTHING which any other human being with similar abilities to yourself had done before; or even something which NO-ONE had done before!

The possibilities are staggering:

You Could Become a Millionaire!

Yes, YOU could become a millionaire! Why not? Millionaires are common! There are tens of thousands of them around the world. It's not so very special. In fact, this is one of the EASIER things to do.

Why do I say that becoming a millionaire is one of the easier things to do?

Well it's obviously not *that* difficult otherwise tens of thousands of men and women would not have achieved it!

There is nothing SPECIAL about these people. Only a small percentage achieved their wealth by inheritance or luck. Most of them are ordinary people like you or me.

They don't all have special abilities or talents which are excluded from you or I. They are not a breed apart, some exclusive elite to which we can never aspire – this might have been true a hundred years ago, but it certainly is not true now. Most of them are honest and hard-working, and they do not have any secret knowledge from which we are excluded.

I became a millionaire in eight years, starting with an overdraft! I promise to you now that I am just an ordinary guy with no special gifts or talents for making money. I wasn't lucky either; in fact I had a lot of bad luck. I just BELIEVED in myself and my abilities. I raised my false ceiling, not to the full one hundred feet but to at least fifty feet! I still have another fifty feet to go!

But having a *fifty foot* ceiling sure as hell beats having a *three foot* ceiling!

Believe me, there is a very, very big difference between having a THREE foot ceiling and having a FIFTY foot ceiling.

Let's All Make Excuses

Perhaps at this point, you are probably thinking things like:

"That's all very well, but......"
"He makes it sound easy, he should see where we live..."
"If it was that easy, everyone would do it."
"I bet he hasn't got children/dogs/sick mother/wooden leg...."

And many other things like this. In fact I hope you ARE making excuses otherwise you shouldn't be reading this book!

Excuses are what people use to cover up or justify their lack of PSI and I-CAN belief.

I hope you will forgive me for calling them excuses, but THAT IS WHAT THEY ARE! I'll show you WHY you feel you have to make excuses and HOW to stop making excuses by raising your I-CAN belief from your present three foot FALSE CEILING to as high as you can go.

I vividly remember the time when I made all sorts of excuses for not achieving success. Do you remember that I told you how I used to blame anything and anybody other than myself?

I blamed my lack of money, I blamed my lack of contacts, I blamed society for favouring the rich, I blamed the depression, in short, I blamed everything except myself!

Why do you think I made these excuses?

Simple! I made excuses because they LET ME OFF THE HOOK!

That's right! It worked like this:- If something else or somebody else was causing my failure then I wasn't to BLAME was I? What could I do about it? It wasn't MY fault. After all, I had all these handicaps like lack of money and lack of ability! "Anyway," I told myself, "what's the point in even TRYING? The only people who make it in this world are either rich to start with, or lucky, or dishonest... and even if I *did* make lots of money, the taxman would take it all, so what would be the point?"

I didn't take responsibility for my own life. It was easy and convenient for me to blame someone or something else for my failure.

Do you see how not taking responsibility for your own life is VERY CONVENIENT? The pay-off is obvious. By blaming external agencies you absolve yourself from responsibility, which, in turn means YOU DON'T HAVE TO TRY ANY MORE.

These excuses were formed very early in your childhood, and they served the purpose of preventing you from having to make changes to your I-CAN World View.

For example, there was a time when you had to struggle to learn the basics of mathematics. Love it or hate it, this level of mathematics CAN be understood, with some effort, by most children. Somewhere along the line you may have learned the neat trick of saying something like: "I'm *useless* at maths, my Daddy and teacher both say so. I've always been useless at it, and I always will be."

This gives you the perfect excuse! If Daddy AND teacher both say so, then you have the approval of high authority for your imagined weakness. The pay-off is obvious. You no longer have to struggle to learn maths (or French, or history, or whatever)! After all, what's the point? You KNOW that you'll never be any good at it.

Note that this hardly affects the PSI-belief (although the two types of belief are intimately connected). You don't necessarily feel bad about yourself over this, you just believe that you are no good at maths – or whatever subject applies to you.

This type of belief is also nicely self re-enforcing – here's how it works:- The more you believe that you are useless at maths, the less you will try, ("What's the point?"), so the worse you will get, ("I told you so!").

Now here is something really interesting:- Our society often gives out POSITIVE strokes to people who demonstrate a *lack* of I-CAN belief, PARTICULARLY TO GIRLS. This is one of the many reasons why women are disadvantaged compared to their male counterparts; they are actively encouraged (albeit by subtle messages), to demonstrate a low level of I-CAN belief.

Here are two fairly typical examples:

JOHN: "I'm useless at maths!"

DAD: "Nonsense son, you'll just have to try harder."

Compare this with:

MARY: "I'm useless at maths."

DAD: "Never mind sweetie, you can't have a pretty face AND be clever at everything can you?"

Going right back to the beginning of this book, do you remember that I told you how I read every 'Positive Thinking' book that I could get hold of, then synthesised my own method?

Well one thing that really struck me after about the fifth book, was that women were totally excluded from these books. In every single book, the reader was always referred to as "he" NEVER "she" and the books were packed full of nice little sexist examples using a boss, (always a man), and a secretary, (always a woman), as the main characters.

Why do I make this point? Because 'Positive Thinking' books are rarely aimed at women. Women are NOT encouraged by our society to raise their level of I-CAN belief. In fact it is definitely frowned upon if a woman appears too capable or appears to believe in herself too strongly (unless that belief is confined to 'safe' subjects like cooking or bringing up babies, and then only as long as the very top chefs and child care specialists are men!). Most women who do possess a high level of I-CAN have long ago learnt the trick of playing it down – especially in front of male associates.

It is not my intention to explore the subject of sexism at length in this book. I am not qualified to do so, and it has been well covered by other authors. I only wanted to use this as an example of how a lifetime of training in lowering a person's I-CAN belief, can result in their being confined under a very low ceiling.

I said earlier that most people are confined under a three foot ceiling; if you're a woman reading this then subtract one foot!

Lack of I-CAN belief EVEN IN ONE OR TWO SUBJECTS is a crippling disease. If you don't take the trouble to correct the problem then WHOLE AREAS of life are forever closed to you. In the case of our example, you may not consider maths to be a great loss, but you would be wrong.

Maths is an amazing, wonderful, subject; you could devote a lifetime to it and hardly penetrate its mysteries. I'm not saying that you should immediately go out and study maths, but it is a sheer tragedy if, every time you brush against the subject, the mental shutters come down and you switch off.

It is TERRIBLE to be crippled like this.

It is the same with ALL subjects. They are ALL intensely interesting; it is only your lack of I-CAN belief which prevents you from finding them so.

When you raise your level of I-CAN belief, it is like raising a curtain on the world. EVERYTHING becomes possible; EVERYTHING is interesting. There is NO SUCH THING as a boring subject; there is nothing which you could not become proficient in, given time.

This does not mean that you have to become a leading mathematician and scientist; play the cello to concert standard, learn nineteen languages and become a respected brain surgeon – but you COULD do any one (or more) of these things if you wanted to. We are not talking here about *doing* all these things, but about allowing yourself to believe that you *could* do them if you decided that you wanted to.

It is this belief in your abilities which signifies a high level of I-CAN. This means that ANY opportunity which comes your way is OPEN to you; not closed by your low I-CAN. You can learn anything you want.

You may not WANT to learn Arabic but you KNOW that you COULD if you wanted to. The I-CAN'T person would say something like: "I've always been useless at languages."

You may not WANT to learn to water-ski but if the opportunity came along, you KNOW that you COULD master it, given time. The I-CAN'T person would say something like: "I'm hopeless at sports; I've always been that way; I'll never change."

You may not WANT to start your own business, but you know that thousands of ordinary people have done just this, and so could you if you wanted to. The I-CAN'T person would say: "It's too complicated; all those figures, I could never do that."

So, we have learnt that due to laziness, the brain learns to make excuses for lack of ability. The pay-off for making excuses is that you don't have to TRY anymore, so you don't have to risk failure. These excuses are self re-enforcing. They lower your level of I-CAN belief and bar you from whole areas of life.

Let me give you one excuse and two examples which serve to illustrate exactly how shallow these excuses can be: The excuse is: "I'm too old/infirm to do anything."

There is a lecturer at Cambridge University who suffers from a crippling progressive wasting disease which prevented him from walking. He wanted to carry on working so he bought himself a wheelchair and continued lecturing.

Then the disease paralysed him so that he could only talk and move one hand. He modified his wheelchair to be operated by one hand and carried on lecturing.

As if this was not bad enough, the disease attacked his voice box which had to be removed surgically. Did he give up? No. He had a friend design a computer linked to a voice synthesiser. He now uses one hand to select from a menu of words from which he constructs sentences and feeds them to the synthesiser. He now carries on normal conversations by means of his computer voice. He is still lecturing.

I still think of this man when I am tempted to moan about my physical problems.

I sometimes go hang-gliding. I thought this was a young person's sport until I found out that one of the champion hang-gliders was over sixty five! He took it up when he was sixty!

A very great many of the famous people throughout the centuries have done some of their best work during their so-called 'old-age'. Age was not a barrier to them, why should it be to you?

How easy it would have been for any of these people to give up, call it a day, say "I'd love to do that, if only...."?

These are just a few of the many thousands of people who have triumphed over the most amazing difficulties. You'll find that the people with the most severe handicaps are often the ones who do the LEAST moaning and excuse-making. It is often the people with quite mild problems, or even no problems at all, who use it as an excuse.

I used to know a chap in a wheelchair who hitchhiked around Europe! Yes...hitchhiked! He would sit in his wheelchair on the verge of the road and thumb a lift! Drivers would be so amazed to see him that they would stop. The wheelchair would be put in the boot, and Stephen would be helped into the front seat.

Where was the problem? He got a lift more easily than able-bodied hikers!

Being too old/young or claiming a physical disability are just two of the many excuses which people make for not achieving the success that they deserve.

When you raise your I-CAN belief, you stop making excuses!

Let's face it, all of us have restrictions which we could use as excuses. We're all either poor, lacking in ability, lacking in opportunity, bogged down with responsibilities, too old, too young, ill, infirm, the wrong colour/race/sex etc etc. The list goes on.

Here are a few of the excuses which people use to justify their lack of success:-

"I never had a proper education."

"The trouble with me is that I'm too highly qualified!"

"It's all right for you, I was in my first job at thirteen, what chance did I have?"

"Mummy and Daddy were very rich, consequently I didn't have to do a stroke! If only I'd been made to get a job at thirteen, that would have given me the toughness which I lack!"

"Everything costs money nowadays. Even if I could think up a good business scheme, I haven't got a penny in capital."

"My problem is I'm too well off! Consequently I just dabble around at things and don't take anything seriously. If only I had less money; I'm sure I would try harder."

To Moan or Not to Moan?

How can you tell an excuse from a genuine complaint? Simple! Excuses are nearly always given as a REASON for inaction. Complaints are just moans and groans; they rarely stop people getting on with things after they have had their moan.

There are other little ways of spotting an excuse, either in yourself or someone else; for example, key expressions often give away excuses. Expressions like:

"If only ....."
"It's all very well but......"
"I could never do that."
"It's all right for you...."

A person uses an excuse to justify why they HAVEN'T done something. If they just outline their problems without using it to justify their inaction, then it is probably not an excuse, just a moan.

For example: "This weather plays havoc with my arthritis," is just a moan, but: "What's the point in taking a holiday in this country when the weather is so awful!", is definitely an excuse.

There is an acid test of an excuse: **If someone demolishes the excuse, is another one immediately offered in its place?**

This is a cast iron test of excuse-itis, caused by lack of belief. For example, here is an imaginary conversation with JERRY:-

JERRY: "I've always wanted to go to Disneyland, but I can't afford it."

ME: "That's amazing! Just this morning I was given an 'all expenses paid' holiday to Disneyland because I met my sales target. I'm booked up for a holiday already, so why don't you go in my place? I owe you a big favour anyway."

JERRY: "Really? Thanks a million. I'll go!"

In this example, Jerry was not using excuses to maintain a FALSE CEILING. He saw an opportunity and seized it. However, supposing the conversation had gone differently and he had responded to my offer as follows:-

JERRY: "Wow! I'd love to go but I get really scared in aeroplanes; it's a real phobia."

ME: "It's your lucky day! This is a *sea* cruise taking in the sights of New York, then traveling by Greyhound bus to Disneyland."

JERRY: "A sea cruise? Hey, won't that mean that I have to be away for over a month? I couldn't do that!"

ME: "Sure you could! What's stopping you?"

JERRY: "What about work? I couldn't take all that time off."

ME: "I'm your boss. Take a month off, you've earned it."

JERRY: "Well you see I have this collection of rare snakes which have to be fed every day. I couldn't leave them."

ME: "Snakes? Hey, I *love* snakes. Do you think I could feed them for you?"

JERRY: "But I'm expecting an offer any day from my agent, I'd hate to be out the country when that call came through."

ME: "O.K. Get him to call you at your hotel."

JERRY: "Her."

ME: "Him; her; what's the difference?"

JERRY: "It's a great offer. Look, I'll think it over and let you know tomorrow."

Build That Wall!

Do you think Jerry will go? NOT ON YOUR LIFE! Did you notice the way he kept inventing a new excuse every time I demolished his previous one? I call this effect the BRICK WALL EFFECT. Not content with having a three foot high ceiling, people also build brick walls around themselves! The bricks are the excuses; one brick for every excuse. Take a brick out of their wall, (by demolishing the excuse), and out comes the trowel and cement and another brick goes right in its place.

When I meet people suffering from acute 'brick wall' syndrome, I like to play the 'brick removal game'. Just like in my imaginary conversation with Jerry, I attempt to remove their bricks one by one and see how good at brick-laying they are!

Some people are expert bricklayers. They're so quick that you can't take bricks out of their wall fast enough to cause a noticeable hole before they have closed up the damage with new bricks.

Other people are a little slower, and you can get quite a few bricks out. These people usually get angry or into a huff; then they'll run away to repair the damaged wall at their leisure!

Here's an example of a conversation with a slow bricklayer:

ME: "You've just said that you can hardly make ends meet; but it doesn't have to be like that. You can earn as much money as you like if you start believing in yourself."

BL: "What are you talking about? I'm unskilled. The most I can earn is £200 a week. You have to be a supervisor to earn more."

ME: "Why aren't you a supervisor then?"

BL: "Why? I'll tell you why, since you're asking. You need to pass your exams to be promoted to that grade. I left school at thirteen so I didn't have much of a chance, did I?"

ME: "O.K. so get your exams at night school."

BL: "At my age? You must be joking! Anyway, I can't study, I'm no good at it, I never was."

ME: "Actually, you'll find that most of the people at the classes will be older than you."

BL: "Anyway, what's the point? My boss hates me so I'd never get promoted."

ME: "Then change jobs."

BL: "You think its easy don't you?"

ME: "No, but if you really want to improve your standard of living, then you'll find a way of getting a better job."

BL: "It's all right for you. I expect jobs are ten a penny where you live. Your sort make me sick trying to tell people how to run their lives!"

At which point he stomps off as he is not used to having his excuses attacked so relentlessly!

Why are people so rarely challenged when they make an excuse?

There are two main reasons for this:-

Reason one: It is considered 'impolite' to contradict or challenge someone, particularly if you don't know them well. For example, this type of conversation would be unlikely to win you many friends:-

JANE: "I'm hopeless at dancing. I've always had two left feet but I'd give anything to learn to dance properly. There's not a chance of doing that because of my responsibilities and lack of money."

YOU: "I disagree. If you really wanted to learn to dance properly then you would find the time and the money."

Whilst what you said was true, Jane would almost certainly be slightly offended by your reply . The "polite" response would have been:

YOU: "Yes, it is difficult to find time when you have a growing family."

This reply subtly re-enforces Jane's negative position.

Reason two: By AGREEING with the excuse-maker, you find a 'partner in crime' who will help you re-enforce your OWN lack of I-CAN. For example:-

DAVE: "This weather is *awful* . My wife wants us to take a holiday but I can only enjoy myself when it's sunny so there's no point is there?"

MARY: "None at all. I would love to have a nicer garden but with the weather we've had, when would I enjoy it?"

DAVE: "Exactly! Speaking of gardens, I've always wanted a swimming pool in the garden, but there's no point if you can only use it for two weeks every year. Anyway, the *price* of them! I'd buy one on credit but I can't budget; I'm useless with money."

MARY: "I know! Everything's so expensive nowadays. I went to the travel agent the other day to see if we could get away for a week, but when I saw the prices I just turned around and came right out! I can never seem to save for things like that, money just slips through my fingers."

DAVE: "If you think holidays are expensive, have you seen the price of new cars recently? I'm sick of driving my old banger so I thought I'd trade it in. I soon forgot that idea when I saw that the CHEAPEST car was...."

And on and on. This secret complicity is absolutely RIFE within our society. In fact, so normal is it to play this game that people think you are REALLY STRANGE, and even get offended if you refuse to play the game with them. If you don't believe me, see if you find either of the following conversations a little off-key – two strangers are talking at a party:-

JILL: "I love ballet but I never go; it's impossible to get tickets, they're sold out months in advance."

DONNA: "That's not true. I often go to the ballet, it's easy to get tickets, you just have to book months in advance."

OR:

JOHN: "I'd love to trade my old car in for a new one, but there's absolutely *no way* I could afford it."

DAVE: "I thought that, but then I knew that I deserved a new car so I went ahead and bought one anyway!"

Jill would probably deduce that Donna was a know-it-all, whilst John would figure that Dave was a narcissistic big-head!

In our society it is considered impolite to be positive!

It's amazing isn't it? People tend to think that you're either showing off, or gloating over your own good fortune at their expense. Being negative is far more socially acceptable because it piles the blame onto external events which are out of your control, then everyone can join in and have a good moan. They can all go away feeling happy because their lack of action has not been criticised – rather, it has been praised.

Which is Which?

How can you tell a lack of PSI-belief from a lack of I-CAN belief?
The answer is that often you cannot.

For example, if someone says to you: "I've always wanted to ride a horse, but animals hate me," they could be suffering from a lack of PSI ("Rich people ride horses, I'm a second class citizen therefore I don't deserve to do this.") or they could have a strong PSI but be lacking in I-CAN belief, ("Animals hate me, they always have done.") or they could have a problem in both areas.

In the examples given throughout this chapter, the excuses could be caused by a lack of PSI-belief OR a lack of I-CAN belief.

The two are fairly closely linked anyway; that is why later in this book I give you methods which will dramatically raise BOTH types of belief together.

There ARE methods which you can use to spot which belief is most lacking:- If lack of PSI is the problem, then the actual excuse will be irrelevant. If you demolish one excuse by argument, another will be put in it's place. The 'brick wall' syndrome is more indicative of lack of PSI belief than lack of I-CAN belief.

However, if the person offers one excuse and sticks to it; then shows an interest when you try to indicate ways in which they COULD achieve success; then lack of I-CAN is likely to be the trouble.

Look at all the different types of I-CAN'T belief there are:

Specific I-Cant's

These I-CAN'T beliefs are unique to the individual:

"I'm useless at sport, I always have been. I was so bad that I was the only person in our school to be excused games permanently."

"History is just not my subject. I switch off when I hear anything historical; it's so boring."

"I can't handle money."

"I'm no good with animals; they hate me."

"I don't have enough intelligence to run my own company."

Sex-related I-Can'ts

This category mainly limits women. Society has trained most women from the cradle to expect a lot less than their male counterparts, so typically they have I-CAN'T beliefs such as:-

"I could never be a company director."

"I could never be a millionaire."

"I'm useless at figures, science, woodwork, DIY, car mechanics etc."

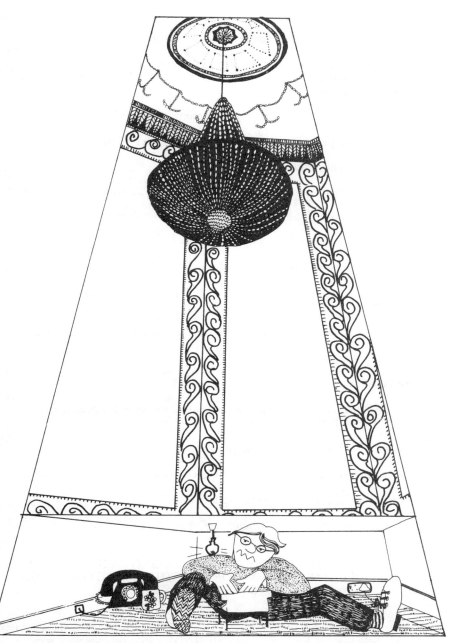

MOST PEOPLE ARE WORKING UNDER A FALSE CEILING WHICH IS LESS THAN THREE FEET HIGH!

"I don't understand a thing about electricity, it's so complicated."

"A woman's place is in the home, not following a career."
"Men need looking after. They can't wash clothes, iron, cook or tidy the house, so I do all that."

Men do not escape from this category! Society has trained them also:

"I could never look after a baby, men just aren't tolerant enough."

"I can't sew, knit, bake, or cook."

"I have no decorative sense, my wife does all that; women are so much better at it."

Race/Regional I-Can'ts

"You have to be white to make it in this town."

"You have to have lived in this village for at least twenty-five years before they acknowledge you."

"I'm a foreigner and can hardly speak the language; what chance do I have?"

Social I-Can'ts

"I never had a chance of a proper education; we were dirt-poor and we all had to go to work instead of school."

"It's not what you know, it's who you know."

"It's easy to make money when you've got money."

"Property is mainly owned by the upper classes."

"It's impossible to get a job around here, there just aren't any."

REMEMBER THAT THE PAY-OFF FOR MAKING EXCUSES IS THAT YOU CAN BLAME SOMEONE OR SOMETHING ELSE FOR YOUR LACK OF SUCCESS.

The secondary pay-off is that CHANGING your I-CAN'T beliefs into I-CAN beliefs takes EFFORT and COURAGE. Your subconscious mind is HAPPY with your set of I-CAN'T beliefs because it feels nice and cosy. Just

The bricks are the excuses; one brick for every excuse.

like with PSI-belief, your sub-conscious will RESIST any attempts by yourself to change it's I-CAN World View.

REMEMBER THAT EVERY I-CAN'T EXCUSE CLOSES A WHOLE AREA OF EXPERIENCE AND OPPORTUNITY TO YOU.

Let's just take one example and examine it in a little more detail. I could choose any example, but I have decided to choose the excuse about men not being able to look after babies. The PAY-OFF for the man is that he avoids some difficult work and does not have to master a whole new set of skills. Every time the baby cries, all he has to do is call for Mum.

He avoids smelly nappies and mopping up vomit because he's "All fingers and thumbs when it comes to doing that sort of thing."

He doesn't have to get up in the night when the baby cries because: "Babies need their Mothers when they are crying, men are too rough."

His additional pay-off is that he doesn't have to radically change his I-CAN'T World View. This is the part of his World View jigsaw which says: "Men are not suited to looking after babies, that's women's work. Women are naturals at it, men are too rough, careless and intolerant. Any man who looks after a baby must be a bit of a sissy; you wouldn't catch me wheeling a pram down the road, what would my mates think? Men just don't have the necessary skills or knowledge to make a good job of it; anyway, even if they did the women would soon be up in arms, it's about the only thing they can do."

To change his I-CAN'T belief into an I-CAN belief, he has to change this whole section of his World View, and there are some pretty major pieces of the jigsaw puzzle contained here. HIS SUBCONSCIOUS WILL RESIST THIS CHANGE PURELY OUT OF INERTIA.

INERTIA RULES THE SUBCONSCIOUS: IT DOESN'T LIKE CHANGE.

Remember, the thought of change produces FEAR which causes INERTIA which tries to prevent the change.

But this I-CAN'T belief closes off a whole area of life experience to the man. Yes, it is very difficult looking after a baby, but it also brings a huge set of rewards which are unique in human experience; ask any mother.

I found out how enriching, (and exhausting), this could be after the birth of our twins. I held some of the I-CAN'T beliefs mentioned above, but there was no room for the luxury of them with twins around! I had to do my fair share otherwise we would never have coped. I soon shook off those old attitudes and I'M VERY GLAD THAT I DID. Yes it was totally exhausting working all day, then going home to a second job. Being woken ten or twenty times a night was the hardest thing I think I have ever coped with, but there is no doubt that I am a better person for it, and I hope, closer to my children.

THERE IS NOTHING WHICH YOU CANNOT DO. THERE IS NO SUCH THING AS BOREDOM. EVERY OPPORTUNITY WHICH YOU SEIZE WILL BRING BIG RESULTS. EVERY TIME YOU SAY "I-

CAN'T" A PART OF YOU DIES.

The Corridor of Life

Imagine life as a long corridor with many doors leading off to each side. Every door is labeled with a particular opportunity, an exciting adventure in life. Behind many of the doors lie success and fortune; behind others are life-enriching experiences. Each door leads to a world of possibilities!

With strong PSI and lots of I-CAN belief, EVERY door is open to you; all you have to do is decide which room to go into and how long to dally there before sampling the delights of the next room.

With poor PSI belief, OVER HALF OF THE DOORS ARE SLAMMED AND LOCKED FIRMLY SHUT, because you don't believe that people like you deserve to go through them. These rooms have gold-plated RESERVED signs on them, and it never even crosses your mind that they may be reserved for YOU!

With lack of I-CAN belief, many of the doors are forever closed to you. Instead of these doors bearing a sign spelling out an opportunity, they each have a large red sign saying DANGER! NO ADMITTANCE.

With so many doors firmly shut, it is not surprising that, after walking down the corridor of life for a while, you begin to wonder why you never get 'the breaks' or why opportunity always seems to pass you by? It is YOU who are passing opportunity by!

After walking down the corridor for a while and trying a few doors, only to find them locked shut, you naturally become cynical; you stop believing that there *is* anything behind the doors at all! This has the effect of preventing you from even bothering to try any more handles!

What Causes I-CAN'T Belief?

It is a learned response. When you were born, you had no pre-conceived ideas about your abilities. All of your I-CAN and I-CAN'T beliefs were painstakingly built up BY YOU over the years.

YOUR ENVIRONMENT DIDN'T LIMIT YOU! You may have had a tough time as a kid, perhaps your parents were very poor, perhaps you were brought up in a slum and beaten every day; but in the end, it was YOU who DECIDED that this would be a limiting factor. After all, THOUSANDS of people had worse backgrounds, yet still made a huge success of their lives. Quite a few even admit that their terrible environment spurred them on the succeed. They knew how bad things *could* be, and they wanted something better.

I agree that it's not EASY if you had a bad environment as a child, but who said it SHOULD be easy? If it was EASY it probably wouldn't be worth doing!

It's no easier for a rich kid. They had everything on a plate when they were children, as a result they didn't value anything or appreciate the good things in life. Consequently they find it hard to succeed because they are used to getting

Imagine life as a long corridor with many doors leading off to each side.

everything they want instantly, so they find it difficult to apply themselves.

Nevertheless, at some point you may have learned that you could use the excuse of your poor environment to great effect. It stopped you trying any more. After all, what could you do? You never had a chance did you?

OTHER PEOPLE DIDN'T LIMIT YOU! Your parents and teachers might have hated you and called you useless, stupid, hopeless and a waste of space, but YOU chose to listen to them and believe them.

They may very well have tried to limit you when you were a kid, BUT YOU'RE GROWN UP NOW! You don't have to listen to them anymore, they can't touch you! The world is absolutely wide open to you, and, if you had a limited childhood then you will appreciate all the exciting opportunities MUCH MORE than someone who is used to being able to do anything they please.

I am hammering this point home because it is VITAL that you understand and believe completely that it is YOU who are limiting yourself with I-CAN'T beliefs, not your ENVIRONMENT, and not other people, but YOU. The ultimate I-CAN'T belief is this:

"I CAN'T succeed because there is nothing I can do about it; it is not under my control. My failure is caused by someone or something else."

Nevertheless, when you were younger, you LISTENED to the people who told you you were useless at sport. You BELIEVED the people who told you that you would never go to college, never make the team, never BE anybody. You valued other people's opinions more than your own. If someone told you that you were stupid, you believed them!

This may be understandable when you were five years old and the person telling you how stupid you were was an adult; naturally you will believe them, and it is at this time that I-CAN'T and PSI beliefs are formed. BUT YOU ARE GROWN UP NOW! You are not five years old any more!

YOU CAN CHOOSE TO ABANDON THESE OLD I-CAN'T BELIEFS.

They are relics, fossils of a bygone time. They are someone else's hang-ups passed on to you. YOU DON'T NEED THEM ANYMORE.

Sure, your subconscious won't LIKE changing the World View. It will HATE throwing away all those nice neat pieces of the jigsaw, it will FIGHT any changes you try and make, but my response is: TOUGH LUCK! Your subconscious WILL change if you use the correct methods. It is like a stubborn donkey, if you are insistent enough, it will walk, but if you are wishy-washy and half-hearted, it will just stand there.

You CAN and MUST change your I-CAN'T belief into I-CAN belief if you are to succeed, otherwise thousands of opportunities will just pass you by. You have to grab EVERY opportunity as it gallops past you if you are to succeed. Blink and it's gone; charging away into the distance until reigned-in by some braver soul.

Without I-CAN belief, you WON'T RECOGNISE opportunity even if it stops and licks your face!

Here are a few invented examples of the sort of opportunity which will pass you by:-

A friend will suggest that you set up a partnership with her and run a book-shop. You want to do it, but will decline because you know nothing about books.
Someone will give you a red-hot investment tip, but since you've never bought shares before and don't know anything about it, you will play safe and not invest.

You will see an advert for a sky-diving course; you want to do it but think that you are too old, or not fit enough, so you don't.

You want to buy your own house but don't think that you can understand the legal/financial technicalities, so you stay in your rented flat.

YOU READ THIS BOOK, BUT YOU DON'T BELIEVE IN YOURSELF ENOUGH TO EVEN TRY MY METHOD. TWO YEARS LATER, YOU ARE STILL IN EXACTLY THE SAME POSITION AS NOW.

So now you know about I-CAN belief. I have told you that I-CAN is about believing in your own abilities as opposed to PSI which was concerned with belief in your own worth. You know that I-CAN is a learned response stemming mainly from the things people said to you as a child. You also know that it is convenient for you to retain these I-CANTs because they prevent you from having to bother to try – and possibly fail.
Having gained your I-CAN'T beliefs, they become a part of your World View, often they become central pieces of the jigsaw. As you know, the subconscious mind does not like changing central pieces of the jigsaw because this causes FEAR and INSECURITY. To prevent you tinkering, the subconscious uses its master weapon of INERTIA. Inertia prevents you from changing.
Clinging onto old I-CAN'T beliefs cripples you and isolates you from many of life's enriching experiences – it effectively prevents you from succeeding. The extent to which your success is inhibited depends upon the type, degree and number of I-CAN'T beliefs held by you, but ALL I-CAN'T beliefs are bad and life-depressing.

In a later chapter I will be explaining my powerful technique for eradicating I-CAN'T beliefs from your subconscious, meanwhile, let's have a look at the third barrier which is preventing you from a achieving everything which you desire.

DO YOU KNOW
WHAT YOU WANT?

6

At the start of this book I told you that I-CAN belief and PSI-belief each contributed twenty-five percent to the secret of success. When you have these, you will be HALF WAY towards achieving everything you want.

But do you KNOW what you want?

This question might surprise you! Up until now, you've probably assumed that you knew what you wanted, it was GETTING IT which was the difficult part! You probably thought, before you read this book, that if you only knew HOW to get exactly what you wanted, then all of your problems would be solved.

Have you ever considered that you might not know what you want? You have probably assumed all along that you DID know!

But the surprising fact is that VERY FEW PEOPLE KNOW EXACTLY WHAT THEY WANT! Oh yes; most people have a vague, woolly idea about where they want to be, but HARDLY ANYONE knows EXACTLY where they are trying to get to, or what they want to achieve.

At best, people have a loosely-formed notion about wanting to "be better," to "improve their finances," or to "succeed," but when questioned, they have almost no idea at all about EXACTLY what they want!

IS IT ANY WONDER THAT THEY DON'T GET IT?

Even people who THINK that they know where they are going, rarely do! It is not enough to say: "I know what I want....more money." EXACTLY how much money do you want? WHEN do you want this money?

It is not enough to say: "I know what I want....a better car." What COLOUR do you want the car to be? EXACTLY which model do you want? By what PRECISE date will you have taken delivery? Will it have a sun-roof, electric windows, leather seats, stereo, air-conditioning? Will it be a manual or automatic?

It is not enough to say: "I want to live in a better house." How many bedrooms/reception rooms/bathrooms will it have? Where will it be located? Will it have a garage/laundry-room/shed/stables/swimming pool? HOW MUCH will it cost?

The Secret Of Knowing

I will now share another secret with you:-

UNLESS YOU KNOW EXACTLY WHAT YOU WANT, (IN THE SMALLEST DETAIL), AND WHEN YOU WANT IT BY, YOU WILL NEVER GET IT.

It sounds hard, I know, but I'm telling you the truth. You will never get it! Why am I so sure? Because if you don't KNOW EXACTLY what you want, then you have nothing to work towards, no specific goals to aim for. You'll just drift along with the vague hope that "things will get better". I know because I did this for years!

Also, if you don't KNOW EXACTLY what you want, then you wouldn't even recognise it if someone gave it to you as a gift!

For example, what chance would you have of arriving at the Hotel Bell Vue, 149 Sidmouth Street, London WC2, if you hopped into a taxi in Glasgow and told the driver that you wanted to get to a hotel, but you weren't sure which one? The chances of you arriving at the correct hotel would be microscopically small!

Put like that, it seems so obvious doesn't it? It hardly seems worth saying that you must know where you want to get to before you can get there! Yet MILLIONS of people go through life unhappy because they "want more", yet they have only the haziest notion about exactly what "more" is!

When, after several years, they still have not improved their circumstances, they blame it on 'bad luck' or say that they never had a chance.

They know that they don't want to be where they are at the moment – so does someone standing on a railway platform! But the railway traveller is clutching a TICKET stating their destination. They know EXACTLY where they are going and so there is a very good chance that they will arrive.

A while ago, I had the following conversation with a friend:-

FRIEND: "I wish I had more money."

ME: "Why, what would you do with it?"

FRIEND: "I don't really know, but things would be so much better with more money."

ME: "How would they be better?"

FRIEND: "Oh, I don't know; I could afford a nicer house, perhaps a better car."

ME: "How much money do you want?"

FRIEND: "Lots!"

ME: "What sort of car do you want to drive?"

FRIEND: "Something better than the one I have at the moment."

ME: "EXACTLY what car do you want?"

FRIEND: "I don't know; I'll have to look around."

ME: "What sort of house do you want to live in?"

FRIEND: "Something larger and in a better area."

ME: "Yes but EXACTLY where do you want to live?"

FRIEND: "I haven't really thought about it."

Do you understand my friend's problem? He doesn't really know what he wants. Small wonder that he hasn't got it!

I cannot over-stress the importance of knowing precisely what you wish to achieve. It is one of the key techniques used in this book to assure your success. Used properly, it will produce almost MAGICAL results.

Let me give you an example of JUST ONE of the many things which I achieved using the method which I will share with you in this half of the book:-

A few years ago I was driving a ten year old Austin mini-van. This car was so badly rusted that it had huge, gaping holes in the wings and sills. As fast as I patched it up with fibreglass, other holes would appear. I could literally push my finger through the bodywork at almost any location!

During the winter, when it rained hard, the car would slowly fill up with water until it was sloshing several inches deep around my feet. I tell you the absolute truth when I say that I had to carry a large plastic cup for a 'bail' which I would use, whilst driving at high speed, to bail water out of the window!

Once, when turning a corner, one of the rear wheels fell off, overtook the car, bounced when it hit the curb, and then landed with a thud on the roof of someone's house! I vividly remember my embarrassment at having to knock on the door and ask for my wheel back! I had to crawl out of their skylight to retrieve it! I then took one nut from each of the other wheels, bolted the errant wheel back on, and was only ten minutes late for the play in which I was performing!

If this story wasn't true, I wouldn't dream of risking your disbelief by inventing such a tall tale.

This all happened at the time I discovered 'goal-setting' as a method for achieving everything I wanted. (I'll be telling you all about goal-setting later on in the book.)

For ages I had wanted a 'better' car. I had absolutely no idea about exactly which car I wanted, I just knew that I was fed up with my existing wreck, so I decided to apply the method I had just learned to see if it would work. Here's what I wrote down on that day:-

"By December 31st 1984 I will be driving a brand new expensive estate car."

I now know that this goal was slightly faulty in that I should have specified the MAKE, MODEL and COLOUR of the car, but it certainly beat my earlier wishy-washy statement of wanting to own "something better" at some unspecified time in the future.

The goal that I wrote was quite good for an amateur! Most importantly it gave the EXACT TIME by which I would have achieved this objective. The detail wasn't too bad either; at least I knew I wanted an estate car and that it had to be brand-new. Later on I'll show you exactly how to write your goals to achieve maximum effect, but "Meanwhile," as they say, "back to the story."

It is important for you to understand and believe me when I tell you that, at the time of writing this goal, I had absolutely no chance of even upgrading my heap of junk into a slightly better heap of junk! I was already heavily overdrawn at the bank, and I had just taken out my first mortgage. It was hurting. I was a bad finance risk, and anyway, I couldn't have afforded the repayments.

I wrote my goal on a piece of paper, along with a few others, and read it out loud twice a day.

The result? Before my deadline date, the company for which I was working started to do really well. As a bonus I was offered a company car within a certain price bracket. I chose a brand-new Ford Granada Estate, top of the range.

I had never owned a car which was newer than five years old before. I drove that car home, feeling like a millionaire. When I got home, I took out my piece of paper, looked at the car, looked at the paper, then looked at the car again. I felt as if a magician had waved a wand! Less than six months after writing an 'impossible' goal, the reality was parked in my drive!

All right, you could argue that the car wasn't really 'mine' but belonged to the company. If you look at my goal, you will see that I wrote "I will DRIVE", not "I will OWN". That was my mistake! But I couldn't have cared less at that particular point. If I had written "I will *own* ," then I am absolutely convinced that I would have owned such a car. I know, because I have written many, many such goals since, and achieved them ALL.

It's All Right For Him

I am always wary about telling specific stories about my own experiences. The reason for this is that you might be tempted to compare my own, unique circumstances, with your own situation.

For example, reading the story above, you might be tempted to comment: "It's all right for him, he was obviously in a job where a company car was at least a possibility. In my job, there is absolutely no chance of ever getting a company car."

These comparisons are very dangerous because they are actually excuses caused by lack of PSI or lack of I-CAN. My circumstances are absolutely unique, so are yours. I KNOW WITH ABSOLUTE CERTAINTY that I could have achieved my goal if I had been penniless and jobless.

Very few people have absolutely nothing at all; no money (I mean absolutely none), no place to live, no talents, no skills; so it is always tempting, when told a success story, to say, "Oh yes, but he at least had so-and-so."

I had my fair share of talents and abilities. JUST LIKE YOU HAVE.

I wasn't destitute, at least I ate regularly, owned a TV. set, drove a car (of sorts) had a HI-FI and records and many other things. I was only poor by Western standards. By Third World standards I was richer than a king! SO ARE YOU!

I know this because almost no-one in our society is absolutely destitute (unless by choice), unlike other countries. Also, you paid quite a lot of money for this book, which means you are at least eating!

Despite all this, the problem kept re-appearing. Every time I talk to people about how I achieve everything I want, they would immediately start to make comparisons between my situation and theirs.

I Confess

For example, I have a university degree in electronics. This is like a 'STOP' flag to some people! You can almost see the RELIEF in their faces when I 'confess' this sin. They immediately seize upon this and say something like: "Oh, you've got a *degree* . Well, of course it's easy when you have a *degree* . I mean you can have your pick of jobs when you've got a *degree* can't you? The pay is so much better; no *wonder* you achieved all those things! Of course it's different for me. People didn't go to university so easily when I was young, anyway I had to leave school at fifteen. If only I had gone to university, things would have been so much better!"

As they walk away I can hear them muttering, "A *degree* , well of course a *degree* makes all the difference..."

As I explained in the last chapter; their reaction is a direct result of poor PSI or lack of I-CAN. It has NOTHING to do with the reality of the situation.

I believe that the negative effects of sharing my personal story with you are outweighed by the positive effect of convincing you that I am just a normal person with a true and exciting story to tell. By telling you about myself, I want you to think something like: "This guy's nothing special! I could do what he's done, and more!" AND YOU WOULD BE RIGHT.

You could say that I got my car because I was in a good job where a car like that was at least a remote possibility. You could say that I was in that job because I had a degree and that I got a degree because I had passed my school exams. But what will you have said?

You will have said that I believed in myself, worked very hard to get my exams, (believe me I didn't find it easy), struggled through university, (I was nearly kicked out), then worked my way up through a career until I was in a job which could support a car like that. What's easy about that? Where's the "free hand-up" which I received and you didn't?

Nevertheless, I was intrigued to see if goal setting could work if you had absolutely nothing – in the Western World sense.

For example, most of the money-making ideas which you might like to try, require SOME capital. Even running a small business from home will mean that you have to fork-out some money to start with. This is the most common complaint (excuse) which people give for inaction: "I haven't got a penny to start my own business!"

When someone from the Western World complains about not having a penny, this usually means that they own a colour television, possibly a video, certainly a HI-FI or record player, a radio and many other luxuries. They also spend quite a lot of money each month on cigarettes, drink, chocolate or other luxury food items.

But I won't go into that!

In Western World terms, I will define a 'penniless' person as follows:-

Someone who has a place to live, can afford the basic necessities of life like food, clothing, and heating (although they have to carefully watch the budget). They own a few luxury items like a television, radio, record player, watch, some jewellery; but none of it is 'worth much' and they cannot afford to go and buy new things very often, if at all.

Their income exactly equals their outgoings. There is nothing left over to save; in fact they are often in debt to quite a large extent through finance, credit cards and bank overdraft.

The possibility of raising, say, £1000 to start a speculative business venture seems like zero.

Does this sound a bit like you? I fitted the above description exactly, before I started to use the Midas Method.

A while ago, I used to suggest to people in this situation that they could find £1000 if they really wanted to – for example, they could sell a few things, cut back on drinking and smoking and perhaps take an extra part-time job for a few months. But I was met with such a hail of excuses and disbelief every time, that I decided to do something about it.

To prove the power of my technique, and purely as an exercise for this book, I wrote the following goal:-

"Starting with nothing, I will make £1000, net of expenses, in eleven weeks. This I will achieve without working for more than 11 hours."

The wording of this goal may seem a little strange, so I will explain. Remember I was starting from NOTHING, so I allowed one week to get my first pound, another week to double it into two pounds, another week to double that into four pounds, and so on, until I had exceeded £1000. (If you do this, you actually end up with £1024.) This takes eleven weeks.

Obviously I could have made £1000 by working in a pub part-time for a year, so I set the time limit of eleven weeks. Also, if I had given up work, I could have earned £1000 in eleven weeks just by working a forty hour week for £2.27 per hour; so I set a limit of a maximum of eleven hours work. One hour a week for eleven weeks.

When I set this goal, I had no idea at all about how I was going to achieve it, to be honest, I found this goal more difficult to achieve than a lot of much larger goals I had set myself. For example, it is much easier to turn £5000 into £10,000 (thereby making £5,000), than it is to start with nothing and make

£1000.

I achieved this goal. If I can do this, so can you. I made my £1000, starting from nothing, in eleven weeks. I didn't work for more than ONE hour in total (as it turned out); that's £1,000 per hour! Not bad going!

Purely for your interest, I will tell you how I achieved this goal although there is a danger that you will dismiss it as 'chance' or 'good luck'. If you set yourself this goal, obviously you would achieve it in an entirely different way.

The first part of the story is so strange that I admit that I was tempted to change it for something which you would have believed more easily, however, working on the basis that truth is often stranger than fiction, I have decided to tell you exactly what happened to me.

The first problem was getting one pound. Actually I had tens of pounds in loose change lying around, but the point was to start from nothing. I honestly didn't know how to get this first pound but I had a 'fall-back' position in that I was going to ask a friend to give me a pound, no questions asked. As it happens, I didn't need to do this.

On the evening of the very first day, I was at a disco celebrating New Year's Eve – right in the middle of the dance floor I found a one pound coin. The amazing thing was that the dance floor was absolutely covered with small round cardboard inserts from 'party-poppers' which had been fired off at midnight. These inserts were exactly the same size and shape as a one pound coin so I was lucky to find a pound coin in the first place, but incredibly lucky to spot it amongst the debris. Needless to say, I wasn't looking for pound coins, I was busy seeing the New Year in. I'm not superstitious, but that really did seem like an amazing sign that things would go well in the coming year.

I was now the proud owner of one pound! I needed to double this into two pounds; again I thought of asking a friend to give me a pound, but again I didn't need to. About two days later, I was walking through town thinking about how I could turn one pound into two pounds when suddenly, there on the pavement before me was another one pound coin! I picked it up in absolute amazement and carried on to the Baker's shop. As I walked into that shop, there, on the floor, was yet another one pound coin!

Not five minutes after finding the second coin, I had found a third – this was getting spooky! I honestly can't remember the last time I found any money before these incidents, so it was not as if I was in the habit of stumbling over money just waiting to be picked up! As I say, this is so odd that I was tempted to invent the start of this story by saying that I borrowed five pounds to get going, but I wanted to share this amazing experience with you.

You may be relieved to hear that I didn't just walk around town and pick one thousand pounds up in loose change from the pavements! That was the end of finding one pound coins – I haven't found one since, but the story has an interesting sequel. Over the next few weeks I kept finding money. Often only one or two pence at a time, but sometimes twenty pence. I must have found over FIFTY coins over a three week period (only totaling one or two pounds), I still have them in a bag at home. It got to be so that I couldn't walk anywhere without finding money – it became a standing joke amongst people who were with me. After I achieved the one thousand pound goal, this phenomena suddenly ceased and I haven't spotted so much as a one pence piece since. Strange isn't it?

So I now had three pounds. As it happened, the following day was my birthday. One of the cards was from my sister, and in it she had included a five pound note as a 'joke' present, we had long ago abandoned sending presents on birthdays so this was really strange. I wondered if including this gift would be cheating, but decided that it had the same strange quality as finding the money, so I decided to add it to the pot – I now had eight pounds for a total 'work' time of about twenty seconds!

Nothing happened for about a week, and I was really struggling to work out how to convert eight pounds into sixteen pounds when out of the blue a friend called and asked if I could get some electronic parts for him since he knew that I had contacts. The interesting thing was that he could easily have got those parts for himself, I don't know why he bothered me about it. I asked him how much he wanted to pay and he said two hundred pounds, maximum (this was for fifty parts). I made one phone call and found the parts for eighty pounds!

Now I must confess that I cheated very slightly here. Since I only had eight pounds legitimately, I couldn't buy those parts for eighty and then sell them to him for two hundred, so I used some of my own money to buy the parts. But I COULD have asked him to send me a cheque for two hundred pounds and THEN I would send the parts, but since I knew he was desperate for these parts I didn't want to keep him waiting for them. I allowed this transaction because although I cheated and used some of my own money, I didn't have to and I could have made the same deal by getting money 'up front'.

To my horror, three complete weeks went by without me being able to do a thing to increase the money, there just didn't seem to be any opportunities. I couldn't think of any way of doubling this money because it was such a small amount. If it had been five hundred pounds, I would have looked for a used car bargain, polished it up and sold it for six hundred and fifty; something like that – but there's not much you can do with one hundred and twenty eight pounds. It began to look as though I was going to fail in this goal but I kept reciting that goal daily, and I truly believed that I would achieve it.

In desperation, in the sixth week I invested that money in some OTC 'Penny Shares', these are shares not traded on the stock market which can show spectacular rises (and falls) in a short period. Over the next week the shares lost twenty percent in value – I was getting gloomy, I only had five weeks left to make over eight hundred pounds! Then I got lucky again and after a further two weeks the shares climbed in value until they were worth two hundred pounds (after deductions). I decided to pull out with the two hundred – time was getting short.

I ought to point out that I know little about shares or the stock market and I am certainly not an expert.

I was now in real difficulty since I had two weeks to make eight hundred pounds – a seemingly impossible task. A further week went by, and again it looked like I might have to abandon the goal; but then another amazing event happened.

Totally unrelated to this, I had been wanting to buy a larger telescope (as I am interested in astronomy). Whilst thumbing through "Exchange and Mart" I saw an advert for a twelve inch reflecting telescope, mounted, with drives for five hundred pounds. This was an absolute bargain and I telephoned the (local) number immediately. The owner had, unfortunately, developed cancer and was unable to engage in his hobby, he just wanted all the equipment cleared out as he was moving to a smaller house. He told me that one person had already called who was on his way to look at it. I ascertained that he would sell to the first person who arrived, and so I immediately jumped in the car and drove round there.

The telescope was housed in a large observatory with a motorised roof and the instrument was everything I wanted. It was also being sold at a give-away price. I immediately wrote a cheque for five hundred pounds and told him that I would collect it sometime over the coming months. He said that I would need to bring a large lorry; this I couldn't understand, as the instrument would have fitted into a modest van. He then stunned me by asking how else I was going to move the observatory! Apparently the observatory was INCLUDED in the price! I couldn't believe my ears! There had been no mention of this in the advertisement and the observatory was worth at least a thousand pounds (as indeed was the telescope).

To cut a long story short, since I didn't need the observatory I sold it for eight hundred and fifty pounds the very next week. This, together with the two hundred pounds made one thousand and fifty pounds; I had achieved my goal – just!

You may think this was a bit of a cheat since my two hundred pounds were not enough to buy the telescope and observatory, but again I COULD have achieved that same result with just the two hundred. I would have used the two hundred pounds as a deposit, then sold the observatory for eight hundred and fifty, used three hundred to pay off the owner, then sold the telescope for at least a thousand pounds thereby making much more than one thousand pounds! It just wasn't convenient to do this, and anyway, I wanted the telescope, the point is that I could easily have taken this route.

This story has one main point – that I achieved the goal I set out to achieve. I wish it had been a little 'cleaner' and more obvious (like buying and selling a few times to build up the money) but it didn't work out that way for me, perhaps it will for you.

Working for less than ONE hour and with total expenses of a few local phone calls and a couple of gallons of petrol, I made over one thousand pounds in under eleven weeks. Do you think I was lucky? Perhaps I was, but I guarantee that I could do the same thing again and again and again if I decided to.

I didn't need that £1000. I could have drawn twenty times this amount out of my bank in cash. That is exactly why I set this goal, to disprove doubters who could point to my large bank balance and say: "It's easy for you to talk, look how much money you've got!" Had I been 'penniless' (as defined earlier), then within eleven weeks I would have had £1000 in cash with which to start a new business – all by working for less than one hour a week!

Note how precisely I worded the goal. This is what I mean by knowing exactly what you want. It would have been useless for me to set a goal like this: "I will get enough money to start my own business."

How much money? £1000? £10,000? When would I get this money? In three weeks time or twenty years? How hard would I have to work for this money?

Money: The root of all happiness?

I have talked a great deal about money in this book. The reason for this is that money is a tangible item, and is also the route to many other things. However, it is important for you to know exactly where you are going in every aspect of your life – financial, emotional, and spiritual.

If you are enmeshed in an unhappy relationship, you can use the principles of the Midas Method to improve your relationship or to get out of that relationship and to find the partner which you deserve.

If you are oppressed by the pace of life, then you can use the Midas Method to ensure that you get sufficient time to meditate or just to be quiet and alone.

With a firm foundation of PSI and I-CAN belief, adding KNOWLEDGE brings you a massive SEVENTY FIVE PERCENT of the way towards achieving ANYTHING you want.

Wanting Too Little

Notice I say wanting too little; not wanting too much!

This is one of the problems you may be faced with when you start to think about exactly what you want. Suddenly, you have to clothe your earlier tenuous ideas with form and shape. Instead of just saying "I want a better house", you have to start thinking about exactly what house you DO want. Where this house will be located, how many rooms it will have, how much it will cost?

The temptation is to set your sights TOO LOW. Guess why? Yes, our old friend lack of PSI-belief tells you that you don't DESERVE to live in anything too grand. Your PSI World-View tells you that people of your class, background, age, or race are restricted to certain types of (smaller, cheaper) houses, but OTHER people, who are BETTER than you, live in the bigger, more exclusive houses.

Your lack of PSI tells you that you are a second class citizen. As such, you are restricted to second class housing. Larger, better houses are RESERVED for first class citizens.

Then again, your lack of I-CAN whispers to you that even if you believe that you deserve such a house, there's no point in setting it as a goal because there is no way that YOU could achieve it. After all, you're poor/badly educated/talentless and can't really do much!

The result is that you set your sights too low. You WANT a large, exclusive, detached house; but you settle for less because your PSI and I-CAN are not strong enough to allow you to achieve more.

This is very dangerous because you will not be happy with the smaller house when really you want the larger house. You will be trying to work towards and achieve something which, at best, you feel indifferent towards!

This means that you won't really try very hard and so probably won't achieve even the smaller goal.

If you really want to own a brand new Porsche 911 then there is little point in setting yourself the goal of exchanging your present ten-year-old Ford Escort for a nine-year-old one! It won't make you happy will it? How can you work towards something which will not make you happy? The answer is that you cannot.

I will be telling you how to set your goals high enough in the second part of this book, but meanwhile, I hope that you are starting to see why it is so vitally important to improve your PSI and I-CAN at the same time as working out where you are going.

Without PSI and I-CAN belief, your best intentions will be sabotaged.

Armed with a solid foundation of PSI belief and I-CAN belief, this KNOWLEDGE of exactly where you are going brings you a huge SEVENTY-FIVE PERCENT of the way towards achieving everything which you have ever wanted from life.

It's amazing isn't it? You can get THREE QUARTERS of the way there without leaving your arm-chair! Believe me; this is true. Some of the world's most successful and powerful people have discovered this secret for themselves:

BELIEVE IN YOURSELF; BELIEVE IN YOUR ABILITIES, KNOW WHERE YOU ARE GOING AND YOU ARE ALMOST THERE!

It sounds easy doesn't it? Well it IS easy, in concept. In practice, you have an exciting challenge ahead of you as I show you how to wrestle with your subconscious in order to get it to change those dearly held beliefs about who you are and what you can or can't do. Don't forget that you will then also have that last twenty-five percent to contend with: GETTING WHAT YOU WANT!

In a later chapter, I'll give you some pointers which will help you with that last twenty-five percent; meanwhile, let us start to explore the powerful techniques which will allow you to achieve your life's ambitions.

OFF YOU GO!

7

You are poised on the threshold of an exciting journey! Once you set foot upon this pathway, you will never be the same person again, because you are about to exchange your old life of failure for a brand-new life of success. The journey will not be an easy one, but the treasure awaiting you will be well worth the effort. The rewards could really not be larger!

This technique can bring you EVERYTHING you have ever wanted, and will want in the future.

Here are just a *few* of the things which you can gain by using this system:-

1. AS MUCH MONEY AS YOU WANT.
2. ANY HOUSE (OR HOUSES) WHICH YOU CHOOSE.
3. ANY CAR (OR CARS) YOU WANT TO OWN.
4. HAPPINESS IN PERSONAL RELATIONSHIPS.
5. SUCCESS IN YOUR PERSONAL ENDEAVORS.
6. A LIVELY, EXCITING, DYNAMIC MIND.
7. TOTAL FREEDOM FROM MENTAL AND EMOTIONAL HANG-UPS.
8. PERSONAL MASTERY (BEING IN CHARGE OF YOUR OWN MIND AND BODY).
9. SERENITY AND PEACE OF MIND.
10. TIME.

Since this method can bring you ANYTHING and EVERYTHING, the list above is obviously not exhaustive – but it's not bad for a start!

I have a pet hate of 'How To Do It' books which tell you all about the amazing results which can be expected, then leave you wondering exactly what *the author* has achieved, (because it is never mentioned!).

I am not going to pretend that I am anything special, or that I have achieved fabulous wealth or world acclaim, that is not the point of this book. The point is to show you how a very ordinary person like me became highly successful within a very short period of time. If I can do it, so can you.

With this in mind, I thought you might be interested to know my current level of progress in relation to the list above. (Remember, I only started to THINK about this system eight years ago; I spent the next six years developing it, and I have only really been USING the system properly for a few years.)

Here is my situation at the time of writing:-

1. **Money:** I have as much money as I want at the moment, although this amount does tend to go up every year! It's amazing how quickly you get used to living on a large amount of money. At least it *seems* large when you first get it, but after a short while, it doesn't seem like very much at all!
   Last year I earned £35,000. I expect to earn £75,000 this year.
   My net assets are hard to calculate exactly, since a lot of my wealth is in company shares. I would estimate my current personal assets to be approximately one million pounds, taking everything into account. Eight years ago, my personal assets were minus several thousand pounds!

2. **House:** I live in an expensive house on a half-acre plot in a high-class residential area. When the builders have finished with it (I'm having five extra rooms added), it will be worth about £250,000 (1987 price!). Not a mansion, I agree, but it is exactly what I want at the moment. I don't actually *want* to live in a mansion; if I did, then I would go and live in one! (They're usually cheaper anyway, after all, who wants the heating bills?)
   Eight years ago I lived in a rented flat.

3. **Car:** I drive exactly the car I want, a BMW which cost £22,000. Later this year I will trade it in for a brand new BMW costing about £30,000. I recently sold my Porsche 911 but I plan to buy a new one in the summer.
   Eight years ago I drove a scrap-yard on wheels.

4. **Personal:** I enjoy great success in personal relationships. When you are happy, outgoing and positive, people naturally like you.

5. **Success:** I achieve almost everything I set out to achieve – and boy do I set myself some high targets! My partner and I built a two million pound electronics company, (started from my kitchen table), in under five years! We didn't have a penny of capital and nobody gave us a helping hand up; it was all done through belief and effort.
   I write books (you're reading one) and poetry. I am a published musician and published playwright. With my new-found leisure time, I expect to get a lot more done in these areas. My plays have been performed several times, and have won "Best Original Play" awards. I am a very good actor and musician, I am learning to fly a powered plane and I also enjoy hang-gliding.
   I could go on and on.
   I am not telling you all this to impress you. We will probably never meet, so that is not my motive. The point is, that less than eight years ago I hadn't done *any* of this, and didn't believe that I could! If it sounds to you like I am a talented all rounder, that is because I AM....now.

Eight years ago I wasn't.

This is exactly what happens when you open the doors of opportunity using the methods which I will share with you. Suddenly the whole world is out there waiting for you – your ceiling is raised to dizzy heights.

6. **Mind:** I have a lively, exciting and dynamic mind. I find ALL subjects interesting, even fascinating.

    Do I like science? Yes, I love it. Art? Yes. Literature? I read anything and everything which comes my way and I am completely without literary prejudice. Tropical fish? Weight lifting? Thermodynamics? Cement technology? Diseases in Gibbons? All fascinating.

    The result is – I am never bored.

7. **Mental Health:** Now this is a big one. I would be lying if I told you that I was totally free from ALL hang-ups. That takes more than one life-time, and results in truly hateful perfect human beings! However, using my method, I have eradicated WHOLE AREAS of hang-ups from my life. It would take a whole book to explain the different hang-ups that exist, and how they screw-up your life, (try "Games people play" by Dr Eric Berne). Suffice it to say that I feel mainly in control of my life and am a happy individual. Eight years ago I definitely was NOT in control of my life, and I was fairly unhappy.

8. **Mastery:** Personal mastery has to do with self-will. Will-power is an essential ingredient to success – it gets things done.

    We all have that novel we are going to write some day, or that company we are going to start; personal mastery gets these things done. It turns chat into action. I can honestly say that I get things done. If I set out to do something, it WILL get done. If I think I will write another play, then six months later it's there, on the table. If I set myself a deadline to write a book (like I had to with this one) it IS completed by that deadline.

9. **Serenity and peace of mind:** It may surprise you to know that this is my biggest goal! It may even amaze you if I tell you that I am not all that bothered about money! Now that I know I can get as much money as I want, I can turn my attention towards achieving peace of mind – a far more valuable commodity! Believe me, becoming a millionaire was a snap compared with the task ahead of me in achieving peace of mind. However, money is a means to an end. We live in an age where time and money are in competition with each other, and the reality is that most people spend almost their entire lives working to earn enough money to live on. I wanted to be free from this artificial limitation in order to have more time to devote to other matters. This I have achieved.

10. **Time:** I work 2-3 days a week 'making money', the remaining 2-3 days I work at creative (non-profit) pursuits. Weekends I spend with my family.

I hope that you will forgive this little excursion into self-indulgence, but it is important for you to know exactly what I have achieved using only the methods explained in this book. A massive SEVENTY-FIVE PERCENT of it was achieved *from my 'arm-chair'* ; in other words, three quarters of it was purely mental; changing my attitudes and beliefs. The remaining twenty-five percent was sheer hard work, dedication and effort! Don't be put off by this last hurdle; the chances are that you are working really hard now, and getting very little reward for it!

I'll be showing you how to work LESS hard and get greater results!

I've told you all these amazing things which I have achieved, but remember this:

MY CEILING IS ONLY FIFTY FEET HIGH, THINK WHAT COULD BE ACHIEVED WITH AN EIGHTY OR NINETY FOOT CEILING!!

How To Do It

This section of the book is concerned with the practical method of how to achieve success.

I will be explaining in great detail, exactly how you can achieve anything you want to in this life. My simple step-by-step method requires only fifteen minutes every day and can be done by anyone, anywhere. The only requirements are a chair and a few minutes of peace and quiet every day.

Wealth Warning

Before we launch into the detailed description of the Midas Method, I would like to issue a word of warning:-

I really want you to succeed; that's why I wrote this book. I KNOW that this method works; I also know that if you try it properly it will work for you too. The problem is that we live in an 'instant' society. Everyone wants results immediately, without putting much effort in. People dabble at this or that for a few weeks without any true will or commitment. One week it's a martial art, then a few weeks of yoga before the latest slimming fad takes your fancy and you give that a try for a few days before giving it up. We buy all the paraphernalia to go jogging but only go three or four times, then we start a correspondence course but don't get past lesson three!

This is the human condition in the latter half of the twentieth century. I could go on to expand on this topic by suggesting that this desire for 'instant everything' causes people to live shallow and unfullfilling lives – but that would be the subject of a separate book! Instead, I'm saying to you that I am offering a method whereby you can gain success and happiness; a method which will take about fifteen minutes every day. You must use it every day for at least three months in order to give it a fair chance. That's only a total of twenty-one hours. Most people watch more television than that in two weeks!

My warning to you is this: Because we are strongly ruled by INERTIA, the temptation will be for you to give up after two or three days. Fifteen minutes every day does not sound like much, but it is amazing how events will conspire to prevent you from finding this small amount of time. Remember, your subconscious mind is working against you at this point, it does not want you to start tinkering with its cosy World View – it knows what you are up to, and it will try and prevent you from achieving your goals.

The first and foremost weapon in its artillery is INERTIA. Here's how it works:- The first few days after reading this book, you will be fired with enthusiasm and raring to go. You will *know* on an inner level, that what I have said to you is true, and you will be keen to start changing your life. You will launch yourself into the daily exercises with enthusiasm and dedication. After a very few days, INERTIA will start to take over. It is rather like a flywheel which you start spinning, after a while it will begin to run down unless you keep putting more energy into it. This is the danger point. You may start to skip the occasional exercise period because, somehow, there just wasn't the time, or something more important came up. Then you skip more and more periods until you get to the point where you are only doing a few exercises every week; then you'll hit a week where you really can't do anything at all....and that will be that – you won't do any more. A year or so later you'll pick this book off the shelf and read it again, wistfully!

IT NEEDN'T BE LIKE THIS!

The answer is to keep ever vigilant. Your weapon against INERTIA is WILL POWER. The two are eternally struggling against each other. The chances of you succeeding are directly related to the strength of your WILL to succeed. I'm not talking about the will required to climb a mountain or get to the North Pole; just the will required to use my system for fifteen minutes every day for a few months. It doesn't sound much, but believe me, it will tax you more than sufficiently.

Everyone (including me) will miss the occasional exercise period. The important thing is not to let it become a habit. If you miss one period, make doubly sure that you do the next one.

Inertia can work FOR you as well as AGAINST you. Once you get that flywheel spinning, it will tend to keep spinning for a while. Similarly, once you get into the exercise habit, you will build a certain inertia which will tide you over times of laziness and indifference.

Above all, always remember that you are playing for BIG WINNINGS. We are not talking about losing a few pounds from your weight, or building up your muscles; the course you are embarking upon will change your life in a profound and positive way. We are talking about YOU being able to get ANYTHING which you want at ANY TIME in the future. Surely that is worth a few minutes every day? But be warned, it won't stop your subconscious trying to trip you up!

End of wealth warning!

The Practical Work

Remember that success is :

25% PSI belief.
25% I-CAN belief.
25% Knowing what you want.
25% Getting what you want.

The following chapters deal with each of these four parts of the formula. You should not really start work until you have read and understood at least the first three chapters; the technique involves raising your PSI, I-CAN and KNOWLEDGE at the same time, therefore you must know about all of the techniques before you start.

I strongly advise you to follow my method TO THE LETTER. Obviously I cannot *tell* you what to do with the information which I am going to give you; all I will say is that the method may not be so effective if you cut bits out or change it around. Without wishing to appear cryptic, I would also say that there are deep and carefully thought-out reasons behind even the (seemingly) smallest and trivial of details, so don't be slap-dash with my method – I know what I'm doing.

In return for following my method exactly, I will guarantee you success! I can do this because I KNOW that if you follow the method accurately and diligently, then it will work for you; just as I know that if you hack it around to suit yourself, then only half-heartedly try it, then it will not work.

So here we go! I promise to raise your ceiling from its present three foot level. How high your ceiling goes depends entirely on yourself; all I can do is show you the method – then it's up to you.

CHANGING "I-CAN'T" INTO "I-CAN"

8

Raise That Ceiling!

Do you remember, in chapter 5, how I told you that most people are trying to work under a ceiling which is three feet high? Just imagine for a moment how confining and stifling this is.

I lived for the first twenty-five years of my life under a false ceiling about this high. Far from believing that I could become a millionaire, I didn't even believe that I could own an *average* car or take a foreign holiday. I'm not talking about a *new* car or an *exotic* foreign holiday, just a five year old saloon and a package trip!

My false ceiling stopped me from learning a foreign language. My excuse was: "I'm no good at languages, I never have been and I never will be." After applying the methods used in this book, I learnt to speak Russian in six weeks! (Very badly, I ought to point out, but enough to know that I could speak it fluently if I wanted to.)

My false ceiling stopped me from going abroad. My excuse was: "It's far too expensive to go to these places, I'll never be able to afford it."

Within the last few years I have spent a month in Papua New Guinea, taken four package holiday trips and visited the U.S.A five times. All of these trips have been holidays, none of them were business. The world is wide open to me, I know that I can go anywhere I want to, providing they'll let me in! Within the next two years, I plan to go to China and Russia, two places I have always wanted visit.

My false ceiling stopped me from earning more than a good living wage. My excuse was: "You have to be lucky or dishonest to make more than a certain amount of money, anyway, I never get the breaks."

This is the single biggest misconception amongst people who want to succeed . They are locked into an illusion of how much they think they *should* earn. This illusion is created by comparing yourself with the other people around you, then *lowering* your ceiling until it matches theirs! Can you think of anything more ridiculous? In my case I was effectively saying: "I can't earn more than £100 per week because Dave across the road is getting that, and he's on a higher grade!"

It is a staggering revelation when you realise, as I did, that this is total nonsense! It is up to YOU to decide how much you want to earn. That's right, just sit down and decide! I did. Forget about other people, forget the flood of excuses which will pour into your brain the moment you attempt this exercise, and, most importantly, forget HOW you are going to do it, just set yourself a level of earnings which you want to achieve.

My level was quite modest, I set myself £35,000 a year. This was all I needed to live very comfortably. I easily achieved this income! Absolutely no problem at all! But, then again, it was quite a *low* income. (If you think it is high, you had better start doing some mental re-adjustment. I believe a high income to be £250,000 a year, and a low income to be anything less than £20,000. I am writing this in 1987.)

I would have a bit of trouble living on £35,000 a year now. This year, I expect my income to be £75,000, but even this I consider to be modest, although comfortable!

Do you begin to see how my fifty foot ceiling beats your three foot ceiling?

My three foot ceiling limited me to driving a beaten-up old wreck of a car. My excuse was: "I couldn't possibly afford a new car." Now I drive the car I want, a BMW worth £22,000. I am just about to trade it in for a brand new BMW which will cost £30,000. This is the car I WANT to drive. I could buy a Rolls Royce if I wanted to, but I don't like them.

My three foot ceiling limited me to thinking that I had to work five days a week, eight hours a day, or more, to earn my living. My excuse was: "Everyone works at least this hard, so I suppose I'll have to."

When you think about it, this is even more ridiculous than limiting your earnings just because: "Everyone else is earning about this much." What is so magical about 40 hours a week? The answer is – nothing! It is a purely arbitrary figure, I don't even know where it came from; yet my World View maintained it to be a fact that you have to work at least this number of hours to earn a living wage. Nonsense!

Some time ago I decided that I wanted to work for about twenty hours a week doing enjoyable and highly profitable work (remember I also need to make £75,000 a year doing this!), the rest of the time I wanted to devote to various creative pursuits; for example writing music, plays and books. My fifty foot ceiling allowed me to do *exactly* this. For two or three days a week I run a profitable business, and the rest of the week is my own to do with as I please.

This is the second most difficult concept for people to grasp. They are locked firmly into the idea that they MUST 'work for a living', even if the work that they do is either pointless, wasteful or even damaging to the environment.

In our society, we believe that ANYTHING is better than fulfilling yourself as a human being. God forbid that anyone should actually sit at home and be creative, or (blasphemy of blasphemies) ...enjoy themselves! Far, far better to be sitting at a factory assembly-line putting tops on talcum powder containers or working in a weapons factory, or producing goods with built-in obsolescence. We believe that people MUST have a job, no matter what that job is. We believe that we MUST while away the greater part of our lives doing something which is totally pointless and which we probably dislike intensely (or, at best, just tolerate).

This 'work ethic' attitude is rife within our society. So strong is it, that I am careful about telling people exactly how much leisure time I have, because they always have trouble with the concept. If I don't particularly want to get involved in a deep conversation about how I run my life, I simply pretend that my business takes up 100 hours a week of my time. People are happy with that, it satisfies their belief that you have to sacrifice everything and work like a demon to earn better than average. If I tell them that it actually takes up only twenty hours and that I make £75,000 a year, then I am in for a long interrogation. The interrogation isn't to find out how *they* can do it too, (I wouldn't mind that and I'd gladly tell them), but the questions are all aimed at trying to prove that I am a liar, or that there is a 'catch' or a hidden secret or that I *really* work far harder and earn much less.

Do you remember that corridor with all the doors of opportunity on either side? Do you remember how I told you that your lack of I-CAN belief had the effect of slamming a lot of those doors shut, then hanging large, red DANGER! – NO ENTRY signs on them?

I've told you about just five of those doors which were locked firmly shut for me. Using my system, I tore the DANGER signs off those doors (and many, many more) and unlocked them forever.

One door led me to the fascinating world of foreign languages. I now know that I could learn ANY language that I want to.

The second door opened the whole world of travel to me. I have been to lots of foreign places now, and fully intend to go to plenty more. I will go anywhere I want to, whenever I want to.

The third door let me set MY OWN salary level. From now on, I decide how much I want to earn. At the moment, that is £75,000 a year, but if I wanted to double, or quadruple that amount, I know that I could.

The fourth door let me choose ANY car that I wanted to own. I chose a BMW, but I could choose a Rolls, Porsche or any other car that I fancy; or more than one if I want.

The fifth door opened onto the amazing, delightful, stupendous world called 'free time'. I now have two or three days a week (apart from weekends which I devote exclusively to the family) to do anything I want to. Amongst other things, I now have time to write books (like this one), I am writing a novel and a fourth play. I compose music and study science. I am interested in astronomy and have my own large telescope; I have an interest in Zen and now have time to meditate regularly for the first time in my life. Needless to say, I take a holiday whenever I want to, and have plenty of relaxation time.

These are just FIVE of the doors that I have opened by raising my three foot ceiling to fifty feet. I have opened dozens and dozens of others, some small, some very large – and remember, I still have fifty feet left to raise my ceiling!

How Did I Do It

Like all the methods in this book, the application is deceptively simple. I say "deceptively simple" because you are likely to be fooled into believing that such simple methods cannot possibly bring the results which I claim. All I can say is that they CAN and they DO. Many successful people use these methods or variations of them, it is now time for you to cash in.

STEP ONE: Watch your language!

I am now going to give you a golden rule which is the essential first step towards removing I-CAN'T from your dictionary:-

NEVER SAY OPENLY THAT YOU ARE INCAPABLE OF DOING SOMETHING

This rule should never, ever be broken. Even if you obviously ARE incapable of doing something (like winning the London Marathon if you are eighty-five years old) there is no need to say so, openly.

This may seem like a small rule, but believe me, it brings BIG results. By observing this rule, you train your subconscious into believing that you can do ANYTHING at all, which indeed you can. Plenty of other people will try to tell you that you CAN'T do something, there is no need to add *your* voice to the throng.

How does this work in practice?

First of all, you have to become aware when putting yourself down in conversation. I used to make negative comments about myself all the time, nowadays, one rarely slips past me without me catching it.

This is the sort of comment that I am talking about:-

"I'd love to enter the London Marathon, but I haven't got the stamina, besides I don't have enough will-power to get out of bed for the daily training."

"Go dancing with you? Have you *seen* me dance? It's not a pleasant sight!"

"Can you do this for me? I'm useless at practical things like that."

How often do you put yourself down like that? Even once is too often! You are going to put a stop to it right now.

Here's a little tip which I used when I first started to watch my language:- Because the negative habit was so ingrained in me, I would often get half way through a self-critical sentence before I realised what I was doing. To stop in mid-flow would have sounded very odd to the listener, so I used to finish the sentence and THEN CORRECT IT. Sometimes even saying the opposite thing, all in one breath! Here's an example:-

"Go skiing with you? have you ever *seen* me do anything like that? I'm absolutely useless at sports (pause)... however, there are plenty of people worse than me and I know that I can learn things quickly, so why not?"

Or:-

"Chess? Sorry, I can't play. (Pause) What am I saying? Of course I can play, I'm probably very rusty but I'll give you a good run for your money."

You won't get away without your comment sounding a little strange, but this won't go on for very long as you learn to catch yourself BEFORE you speak the damning words.

I ought to clarify what we are trying to achieve. You don't have to DO anything which you don't want to do. In the skiing example, if you genuinely don't want to go skiing because you have something more exciting to do, then this method doesn't mean that you have to go. It DOES mean that you go if the only thing holding you back was lack of I-CAN belief. It also means that regardless of whether you want to do the thing or not, you NEVER put yourself down, or use an I-CAN'T excuse as a reason for not doing it.

Here's how to respond if you genuinely don't want to go:-

"Skiing? I'm useless at anything like that. (Pause) Actually, that's a lie, I'm as good as anyone else when it comes to sport; I'd love to come but I've already booked up for this amazing week of yoga......" (Go on to describe the course you have enrolled for.)

Never use phrases like these:-

"I can't...."
"It's all right for you but..."
"I could never do that..."
"If only...."
"I never had a chance..."

Instead, say things like:-

"I can..."
"If he/she can do it, so can I..."
"I could do that..."
"Look at all the opportunities open to me.."

Again, these things SOUND simple but they really are effective. It only took me a few weeks to radically change my negative speech habits into positive ones. I still say the occasional negative thing, but I am ALWAYS aware of it and make the effort to correct it. I now have a slight advantage over you because, having written a book like this, everyone will expect me to be positive for every waking moment of my life; woe betide me if I let the odd negative comment slip out!

When I started to apply this technique I was totally amazed at how often I was being negative about myself and the situation, without even realizing it. In the beginning I had to correct myself about five times a day! Now it is about once a month.

STEP TWO: Take Responsibility For Your Own Life!

Here is another golden rule:

NEVER, EVER BLAME ANYTHING OR ANYONE ELSE FOR YOUR MIS-FORTUNES.

In other words:- Get out of the blaming habit.

This rule should never be broken. Even when you obviously CAN blame something else – for example if your house is struck by lightning and burns down.

This rule should never be broken even if it obviously IS someone else's fault – for example if the bank transfers all of the money out of your account, then claims that it was never in there! (Although you obviously DO blame them when you write and point out their error!)

These times will be very few and far between, and people will admire you for not ranting on about how everyone else is a fool and how God has a personal vendetta against you.

In the vast majority of cases, blaming external circumstances is an EXCUSE which you use to prevent you from taking ACTION which will change your life. Remember, I did this all the time, so I'm not telling you anything which I haven't experienced myself.

Start taking responsibility for your own life – NOW. Change the way you think and act. Don't blame other people, don't even blame yourself, just pick yourself up and get on with it. Put your loss down to experience, and remember that no-one ever achieved anything in this world without set-backs.

Do you think that God is personally against you? Do you believe that Lady Luck always turns away from you? Forget it! You have your share of good and bad breaks, just like me, but the difference between success and failure is *recognising* the good breaks (by opening yourself up to opportunity), and *not dwelling* on the bad breaks. Certainly you should NEVER let a bad break stop you from trying all the harder.

Again, watch your language! This is important. Don't use expressions like:

"You make me sick."
"You make me really angry the way you argue with me."
"You make me feel bad when you don't come home until late."

Nobody MAKES you do anything! This has been true since you moved out of your parent's home. YOU choose to put yourself in certain situations, YOU choose to feel or react in a certain way.

Here are some alternative expressions:-

"I make myself feel sick in certain circumstances."
"I allow myself to get angry when you argue with me."
"I choose to feel bad when you stay out late."

If they sound strange to you, that only goes to show how common it is to blame other people for the way we feel.

Take responsibility for the way you feel, the way you act and the way you are. When you do that, suddenly it is all under YOUR control and it is no-one's fault but your own if you stay the way you are.

STEP THREE: If you're not doing anything more important, grab this chance.

This rule allows you to break free of inertia. Too often we turn down opportunities which come our way even when we haven't got anything else to do.

THE MORE THINGS YOU DO, THE MORE THINGS YOU WILL ENJOY.

I make it a policy to say "Yes" to everything, if I haven't anything better to do. Even if I have no interest at all in the subject, I still say "Yes" in the hope that it will prove to be of some interest. The result is that I am rarely disappointed. ALL subjects are interesting if approached with the correct I-CAN frame of mind.

Think of something which you find boring; opera perhaps, art galleries, physics or maybe history. Now ask yourself an honest question: When was the last time you gave the subject a chance?

If you hate opera, when did you actually last *go* to an opera?

If you find physics tedious in the extreme, when was the last time that you actually watched a documentary, or read a modern "Physics for the layman" type of book? I know what the answer will be – "A very long time ago." In some cases, you won't even be able to remember because it was so long ago.

How do I know this? Because these are *learnt* I-CAN'T responses, often stemming from your early childhood. At one time, you found physics difficult or boring (perhaps through the fault of a bad teacher) and you switched off. You slammed the door firmly shut and hung your own NO ADMITTANCE sign on it. From that day onwards you never gave the door a second glance, you expunged the subject completely from your world.

When you were younger, you were possibly forced to watch an opera on television, and hated every moment of it; opera has little appeal for the under-twelves. From that day on, you closed the door on the whole subject, locked, bolted and barred.

The PAY-OFF is that you don't have to bother to grapple with something which is a bit intellectually stimulating. It is far EASIER to say: "Oh that's boring, I'm not interested in that."

If you follow the rules given in this chapter, you will, like me, totally eradicate boredom from your life. I can honestly say that I am never bored. I find ALL subjects interesting. Even a book on left handed spiral-nut-inserts can be interesting if you approach it with the right frame of mind! (Although you have to be pretty desperate!)

Say "Yes" to every possible opportunity and you will be amazed at the results. Whole new corridors of doorways will be opened up to you, 'chance' will come your way much more often than it comes to other people because you are exposing yourself to so many more opportunities; this way you make your own 'luck'.

I have a standard reply which I give to people who tell me I'm lucky. The reply isn't original, but it is apt. I say: "Yes, I am lucky, but the really funny thing is that the more I try, and the more effort I put in, the luckier I get!"

Now is the time for you to start making your own luck.

STEP FOUR: Say it – believe it!

I am now going to explain a vital practical step for totally eliminating I-CAN'T from your vocabulary. This method is a powerful aid to boosting your I-CAN belief and will open hundreds of doors for you – it certainly worked wonders for me. (Note: You will not be able to put this method into practice until you have read the next chapter on goal-setting.)

Here's what to do:-

Take a piece of clean, white card about the size of a postcard; (in fact a completely blank postcard is ideal). Using a good quality pen (not a ball point, or pencil), write, in your very neatest handwriting, the following messages to yourself:

I CAN ACHIEVE ANYTHING I WANT TO. THE WHOLE WORLD OF OPPORTUNITY IS OPEN TO ME.

EVERY DAY I AM BECOMING MORE POSITIVE. I AM ELIMINATING NEGATIVE THOUGHTS AND FEELINGS.

This is called your 'I-CAN goal card'. Keep it safe until you have completed the book.

I will be giving a full explanation of how to set your goals in chapter 9, but in order not to keep you in suspense, I will explain how to use this card now.

Twice a day, at your appointed time, and at your appointed place (see chapter 9), you will take this goal card and repeat out loud what is written thereon. After each reading you will then strongly VISUALISE the following:-

Vividly see yourself walking down a corridor with many doors leading off on each side. Each door has a sign describing an opportunity or a life-enriching subject, for example: "HIGH SALARY", "SUCCESS IN LOVE", "WEALTH", "MUSIC", "ART", "SCIENCE", "SPORT", "LITERATURE", "BUSINESS SUCCESS".

As you walk past each door, see, in your mind's eye, the door swinging open and revealing a glittering, sparkling world. Feel the excitement each time a door opens. Allow some doors to remain closed. See the DANGER – NO ENTRY and RESERVED signs on the door. Now mentally tear those signs down. Smash them on the floor and stamp on them. Now see those, hitherto locked doors swing open like the others.

This entire exercise need only take about three minutes twice a day.

I cannot overemphasize the powerful effects which such visualisation can have. DO NOT DISMISS IT AS NONSENSE WITHOUT FIRST TRYING IT!

If you have never come across goal-setting and visualisation before, then you are in for a surprise – the effects can be startling! If, however, you are thinking: "Oh that old stuff, I've heard all that before," then I would ask you to suspend your cynicism and actually *try* the system. ANYONE who has given this method a fair chance KNOWS that it works, most people who ridicule it have never even tried it, or at best they made a half-hearted attempt at it some years ago.

If you don't believe anything else I say, please believe me when I tell you that this method WORKS. Thousands upon thousands of people have discovered for themselves the effect that goal-setting and visualisation can have, and these effects are dramatic.

Tackling Particular I-CAN'Ts

The method I have just given you is a general method for increasing your I-CAN belief. This method, used in conjunction with step one and two WILL bring a powerful change in your life; I absolutely guarantee it.

You can use exactly the same method to tackle a particular I-CAN'T which has been holding you back from the success which you deserve. As an example, supposing you are being barred from promotion because the next grade demands a reasonable ability with figures. Your I CAN'T belief has always said:

"I'm hopeless with numbers. I can't even add up my own wages, I can't help it, I've always been that way."

Here's how to use my method to smash this I-CAN'T belief to pieces:- Add to your list of goals (see chapter 9) the following goal:

"I used to be no good with figures, but that is changing. I can easily understand numbers and accounts if I try. By July 1st I will have read and studied enough to easily make the next grade. I used to think that accounts were boring; I now find them very interesting and challenging."

Obviously you will re-word this to suit your particular case.

Now, during the exercise period (chapter 9), visualise yourself studying accounts books and understanding everything. Conjure up a feeling of excitement when you imagine yourself working with numbers and figures; see yourself going for the job interview armed with your new skills – and getting the job.

These goals are called 'I-CAN GOALS' and are targeted at specific stubborn doors which remain closed to you. This power-charged technique will blast those doors open for you in a very short space of time.

How Does The Method Work?

In an earlier chapter I told you how I-CAN'T belief is built up through learned experiences. At some time in your past, you found particular experiences a bit painful so you shut them out. From that day on, you refused to examine the topic again, even though you were only a few years old when you took this life changing decision! Ever since that date, you have been telling yourself that you are no good at that particular subject, or that you have no skill in a particular area, or that you are bored by certain things.

You have been telling yourself over and over again how you CAN'T do a certain thing. Well.... the antidote is simple – you start telling yourself over and over again that you CAN do anything you want. This is what the repetition of your goals achieves.

If this were the only technique available in your arsenal, it could take you ages to un-spin the web of negativity. Fortunately you have a powerful secret weapon – VISUALISATION.

Visualisation has the same effect on goal-setting as turbo-charging has on a car! Every time you visualise your goals coming true, it is like pressing a large red 'BOOST' button. Your progress will be so rapid, you will be pushed back into your seat!

A goal is a carefully worded statement of exactly what you want. The next chapter tells you how to set and achieve your goals.

QUIZ

Before we go any further, it would be useful if you would complete the following quiz. We will be using the results later on when we come to the practical application of the method:-

Question one:

To what extent do you think you could increase your yearly income?

a) Not very much.
b) Trying hard I could probably double it.
c) I could earn 5 or 6 times my present income if I really wanted to.
d) I could be in the top one percent of income earners if I decided that this was what I wanted to do.

Question two:

When was the last time you had a holiday?

a) Within the last 12 months.
b) Within the last 2 years.
c) Within the last 5 years.
d) More than 5 years ago.

Question three:

Do you wish you could drive a better car?

a) I don't drive a car but wish that I could.
b) Yes.
c) No, I drive exactly the car I want. If I wanted a better car, I would go out and buy one.

Question four:

How much time do you spend doing the things *you* want to do?

a) Hardly any; there are just too many other demands on me.
b) Not as much as I would like.
c) Quite a lot.
d) I take as much time as I think I need.

Question five:

Is there a place that you have always wanted to visit?

If Yes, answer question 5b
If No, answer question 5c

Question 5b:

Why have you not gone there?

a) I just can't afford it.
b) I have too many responsibilities.
c) Other people get to go to those places, not me.
d) I am going soon.

Go on to question six.

Question 5c:

Why don't you want to travel?

a) I'm quite happy here at home.
b) I've been everywhere I want to go.
c) I don't much care for foreign countries, no place is as good as home.

Question six:

Are you happy with your love life?

a) No. It could be a lot better.
b) What love life?
c) I'm neither unhappy or happy.
d) Yes, happy.

Question seven:

Do you deserve to travel first class?

a) Yes.
b) Yes but I will never be able to afford it.
c) No, other people do that.

85

Question eight:

Earlier on in this book I stated that you could get anything you wanted just by believing in it. At this stage, what do you think of this idea?

a) It makes a lot of sense. It backs up everything I've secretly believed for years.
b) It sounds interesting, but I don't quite believe it.
c) I have to say that I don't really believe it at the moment.
d) I don't believe it and it will take a lot to convince me.

Question nine:

When you go out to a show (theatre, opera, concert, rock- band etc.) do you buy:

a) The most expensive seats.
b) Expensive seats.
c) Medium priced seats.
d) Cheapest seats.
e) I never go to anything like this.

Question ten:

How often do you 'treat' yourself?

a) Too often!
b) Hardly ever.
c) Now and then.
d) Never.

Question eleven:

How easy would it be for you to work half a week and yet earn twice the amount of money you would expect to earn in a full week?

a) Impossible.
b) It may be theoretically possible, but I don't see how.
c) I suppose it could be done.
d) Quite easy, if I put my mind to it.

Question twelve:

Could you learn to fly an aeroplane?

a) Yes, given time and money.
b) I doubt it, I'm not very good at that sort of thing.
c) No.

d) I'm not sure, but I'd give it a try.

MARKING

On a sheet of paper, label two columns **P** and **I** .
Mark your scores in the two columns labeled **P** and **I** .
Put the score indicated after your chosen answer, in the correct column. For example if your answer carries a score of 5P, put 5 points in the P column; if your chosen answer carries a score of 3I, put three points in the I column. Scores like 2P,3I mean add two to the P column and 3 to the I column.

Question 1	a) 5I. b) 3I. c) 2I. d) 1I.
Question 2	a) 1I,1P. b) 2I,2P. c) 3I,3P, d) 5I,5P.
Question 3	a) 3I,3P. b) 4I,4P. c) 1I, 1P.
Question 4	a) 4I,4P. b) 3I,3P. c) 2I,2P. d) 1I,1P.
Question 5b	a) 4I. b) 3I,3P. c) 4P. d) 1I,1P.
Question 5c	a) 2I,2P. b) 1I,1P, c) 3I,3P.
Question 6	a) 4I,3P. b) 5I,4P. c) 3I,2P. d) 1I,1P.
Question 7	a) 1I,1P. b) 3I,1P. c) 1I,3P.
Question 8	a) 1I,1P. b) 2I,2P. c) 3I,3P. d) 5I,5P.
Question 9	a) 1P. b) 2P. c) 3P. d) 4P. e) 4P.
Question 10	a) 1P. b) 3P. c) 2P. d) 5P.
Question 11	a) 5I. b) 4I. c) 2I. d) 1I.
Question 12	a) 1I. b) 4I. c) 5I. d) 2I.

Add up the total points in the P column and add up the total points in the I column.

Scoring

The **P** column indicates your present level of PSI belief. The *lower* the score the *higher* your PSI belief.

The **I** column indicates your present level of I-CAN belief. The *lower* the I-CAN total, the *higher* your I-CAN belief.

PSI-belief

Look at the total number of points in your P-column.

10 points or less: Congratulations, your PSI level is extremely high and you have a very good image of yourself. You probably feel that you *deserve* all the good things in life, but you don't quite know how to get them. You can afford to do a lot less of the exercises concerned with boosting your PSI-belief and concentrate more on the I-CAN (check your I-CAN score below) and the goal-setting exercises. You are already well on the road to success.

11 to 23 points: You have quite a high level of PSI and basically think that you are a worthwhile person. Your PSI could still do with a boost though, so I would recommend that you did the exercises in the chapter on improving your

PSI-belief. Depending upon how low your score is (within this range), you might be able to do less on this chapter and more on I-CAN and goal-setting.

24-30 points: Your PSI-level is dangerously low; this is probably one of the main reasons that you are not achieving the success you deserve – I know you deserve it, but you're not too sure!

Don't worry, my method is aimed precisely at people like you; don't forget I started with a very low PSI. Pay particular attention to the chapter on boosting your PSI; the methods there will bring big results for you.

31 to 40 points: Let's not mince words, your PSI is at rock- bottom. You don't believe that you are worth very much at all, you don't think that you deserve to succeed, that's why you aren't succeeding! Get to work on the powerful techniques given in the chapter on boosting your PSI and you WILL increase your PSI to a level where you can start to succeed. My PSI was very low when I started, and I managed to increase it by a huge amount. If I can do it, so can you!

I-CAN belief:

Look at the total number of points in your I-column.

10 points or less: Congratulations, you have a strong belief in your ability to do things. No challenge is likely to throw you because you know that you can do almost anything you set your mind to.

Because of your high level of I-CAN belief, you need not spend quite so much time on the exercises for improving your I- CAN. Instead, you can concentrate more energy on raising your PSI (depending upon how you scored) and setting goals.

You have a head start on the road to success.

11-25 points: You have quite a high level of I-CAN belief. You are prepared to tackle most challenges, but there are still quite a few which you will shy away from due to deep seated I-CAN'TS. Depending upon your score, you will need to spend some time on the I-CAN exercises, but you can afford to spend more time on raising your PSI and setting goals.

26-34 points: Your level of I-CAN belief is quite low. There are many things which you think you cannot do, even though there is no logical reason for this belief. Don't worry! The system outlined in the chapter on I-CAN belief will boost your level of belief to a point where you can start to achieve anything you set your mind to.

Pay particular attention to the exercises designed to boost your I-CAN belief.

35-45 points: You have an extremely low level of I-CAN belief. It is probably this factor which is mainly holding you back from the success which you deserve. You do not believe in your own abilities and so your opportunities are severely limited to a small handful.

You must start work as soon as possible, using the techniques which I give you in the chapter on improving your I- CAN belief. My belief was very low when I started to use this system, now I believe that I can do *anything* which I set my mind to. If I can change so radically, then so can you.

SUCCESSFUL GOAL-SETTING

9

Successful goal-setting brings almost magical results!

Do you remember how I told you about getting my first brand-new car? This was my first experience of the awesome power of goal setting. I was amazed that it could provide such huge results so quickly. It wasn't 'luck' either, because I have since used the technique many, many times to get exactly what I want from life.

It is not a new technique. Thousands of successful people use it in one form or another; they have all discovered the immense power which can be unlocked once you KNOW where you are going and KNOW what you want.

> IT SEEMS AN EASY TECHNIQUE. DON'T LET THAT FOOL YOU
> INTO BELIEVING THAT IT CANNOT WORK.

The technique which I will share with you in this chapter seems innocently easy. It is, in fact, an immensely powerful method which will GUARANTEE results if you use it in the way that I tell you.

What Is Goal-Setting?

It is a simple method of WRITING DOWN exactly what you wish to achieve, READING IT OUT LOUD at regular intervals, and VISUALISING the goal coming true.

> ALL THREE OF THESE THINGS ARE ESSENTIAL IF THE
> METHOD IS TO WORK.

Here is the method which I have found to work best. I guarantee results if you follow this method EXACTLY. If you think you know better and decide to skip some parts, or take short cuts, then I wish you luck but cannot guarantee that it will work.

I strongly suggest that you follow my method to the letter. It is well tried and tested, and WILL bring results.

Here's how to do it:-

STEP ONE: Writing Your Goals

The wording: This is all-important. A goal can succeed or fail on the exact detail of the wording. Remember my goal which said "I will *drive* a brand-new car," and not "I will *own* a brand-new car?" Fortunately I didn't mind the mistake at the time, but it could have cost me dear!

This is how to word your goals:

RULE 1: For goals concerning personal improvement; write your goal as though it were happening already.

For example:

"I am becoming more positive in every area of my life; I am eliminating negative thoughts and feelings."

"Every day I am becoming less selfish. I feel more generous towards others and wish to share my good fortune with them."

"I am becoming less irritable. Things do not annoy me as much as they used to."

"I am becoming less dogmatic. I try to see the other person's point of view."

"I used to think that I couldn't learn languages. That is changing, and every day I find it easier to study and understand the German language."

"I used to believe that I was useless at sport. That attitude is now behind me and I am more than willing to participate in any sport which comes my way. I like sport; it is exciting and healthy."

The WRONG way to formulate a personal improvement goal is as follows:

"I will become more positive in my outlook on life."

This is WRONG because it is always at some undefined future time that this will happen. The subconscious is lazy and answers such an assertion with: "Will you? How interesting. O.K., wake me up when it happens!"

Another WRONG way to formulate such a goal is as follows:

"By December 31st 1990, I will be more positive in my attitude towards life."

This is WRONG because personality changes are gradual and do not happen suddenly at midnight on December 30th. It is because personality changes are gradual that you can get away with saying: "Every day I am becoming a more positive," without the subconscious calling you a liar!

The other reason why this example is WRONG is because there is no end to how much you can improve your personality; therefore there is no cut-off point. You can't say: "By December 31st I will be generous." How generous? There is really no limit to the amount of generosity which you could display. That is why it is better to say: "Every day I am becoming more generous," this way you can stop using the formula when you feel that you are generous enough!

You CAN say: "By December 31st I will have changed jobs," because that is a definite, realisable goal with a distinct cut-off point. By that date, you either have, or haven't changed jobs, there is no argument about it.

This leads directly onto:

RULE 2: For all goals other than personal improvement, specify the EXACT nature of the goal and state a DEADLINE by which the goal WILL have been achieved.

For example:

"By February 10th, 1990 I will own a brand-new Porsche 911, bright red with leather seats."

"Starting with £1000, I will make £50,000 net profit within two years."

"By June 1st this year, we will have moved into a four bedroom detached house with large garden. This house will be located in the Richly area of Westerham."

"By next Friday I will have asked the boss for a rise."

"On Sunday I will take the kids on a fishing trip."

"By December 31st, 1992, my net assets will be in excess of one million pounds."

The WRONG way to formulate such a goal is as follows:

"I own a brand new Porsche 911, bright red, with leather seats."

The subconscious will be most intrigued by this blatant lie and say: "No you don't!", before it goes back to sleep!

Several books which I have read recommend this method of stating a goal AS THOUGH IT HAD ACTUALLY HAPPENED. They explain that it makes the event more real. I disagree. It is such a blatant lie to say that you already own something which you do not, that the subconscious will either refuse to believe it, or it may even answer: "You do? O.k. Well done! You won't be needing me then, will you?!!"

To summarise this important rule:

For personal improvement, write the goal as though it were *actually happening.*

For all other goals, describe the goal exactly, and set a *deadline* by which the goal will be fulfilled.

How Many Goals Should You Write?

You *can* write as many as you like, covering all areas of your life, but in practice, I like to restrict myself to a maximum of six goals at a time. This is a handy number without involving you in great long lists, or hours of recitation morning and night – this can become tedious and put you off.

Also, I can remember six goals off by heart. This is useful for times when I haven't got my written goals with me. I also like to recite them at odd spare moments; driving the car is an excellent time for goal reciting – and gets you some strange looks from other motorists!

When I have achieved one goal, I write another. This is like getting a little reward! When one wish has come true, you get to make another. Not bad!

What Goals Should You Write?

I thoroughly recommend that for this first session on goal setting you restrict yourself to the two goals I suggested in the last chapter on boosting your I-CAN belief, and three or four other, simple, achievable goals.

Don't be impatient at this stage and start writing goals to get a million pounds. You *can* get a million pounds using this method, (I did) but wait a few weeks until you have got some positive results from simple goals. This step-by-step approach gives you confidence in the system and stops you getting bored – then giving up. I don't want you to give up, I want you to get everything which you desire by using this system. I KNOW it can be done.

What do I mean by simple, achievable goals?

Well, I would suggest that you set two or three goals of a fairly mundane nature, and one of a slightly more challenging nature.

To find mundane goals, look around the place where you live and choose some irritating job which you have been putting off for ages.

Here are a few examples:- Putting up that shelf you bought three months ago. Fixing the catch on the cupboard that annoys you every time you go to open it. Phoning a friend and asking for the return of that book which you lent to them. Finding the time to visit your sick Aunt/friend/neighbour. Joining the local library.

Slightly more challenging goals would include:-Asking the boss for a rise. Taking a weekend or day break to a town which you have always wanted to visit. Enrolling for a course of driving/tennis/hang-gliding/ballooning lessons. Starting a correspondence course.

Here is a typical example of how your first goal-list might appear:-

"I can achieve anything I want to, the whole world of opportunity is open to me."

"Every day I am becoming more positive, I am eliminating negative thoughts and feelings."

"By next Friday, I will have phoned Mary and asked for the return of my book."

"By Saturday 13th March (two weeks away) I will have repaired the faulty catch on the kitchen cupboard."

"On Monday 15th March, I will meet with my boss to discuss possible promotion opportunities within the company."

"By Tuesday 16th of March, I will have booked a weekend holiday for us both in Scotland."

Don't worry if this list seems mundane! You're only going to be using it for two or three weeks. At the end of this period, you will have tidied up two irritating jobs which have been bugging you for ages; put your mind at rest about your promotion prospects in the company, AND booked a short break. That's not too bad is it?

The goals which I have suggested are only meant to indicate the *level* of goal which you should aim for. I'll leave it to you to decide on the exact detail of the goals.

When you find out FOR YOURSELF that this system WORKS for small goals, you will start applying it to larger and larger goals.

STEP TWO: How To Write Them Down

This may not sound important, but I repeat that EVERY STEP of this system must be followed exactly. I cannot emphasise this too strongly. You may not understand some of the reasons behind my method, but that doesn't matter. What matters is that it works and can get you anything you want.

Spend some time thinking up four or five small goals of the sort that I used in my example; don't forget to include the goals which boost your I-CAN belief.

Now write out your goals roughly on a piece of paper, making sure that you word them as shown in RULES 1 and 2. At this stage, you can cross out words and correct as required. You should end up with a final list of goals, worded exactly as you want them to be, although at this stage, they might look a bit scruffy. Don't worry as long as they are all there and the wording is exact.

Put this paper to one side for the moment.

You will now need a piece of WHITE, CLEAN card. A blank postcard is ideal. Anything about six inches by four inches will do, as long as it is CLEAN and WHITE. A scruffy bit of grey card simply will not do.

Using a good quality (preferably fountain) pen, NOT a biro or pencil, I want you to write the following goal onto the card, in your very neatest handwriting:

On...........I will get up at ....a.m. and write my goals. This I will do without fail.

94

Underneath this write: **My normal getting-up time is.......**
I have left blank spaces in my example, but you should fill them in as follows:
First of all, write your normal getting-up time in the space provided. Let's assume that this is 7 a.m. In the second blank space write a time TWO HOURS earlier than this. In our example, this will be 5 a.m. Now pick a date when you will get up at 5 a.m. to write your goals. Write this in the first space.
Your finished card should look something like this:

On Thursday March 14th I will get up at 5 a.m. to write my goals. This I will do without fail.

My normal getting-up time is 7a.m.

The date you choose should ideally be about five days hence, although anything between three and ten days is acceptable.
This card is called your 'goal card'.
Put this card aside for the moment, with the paper on which you have written your goals.
Now take another piece of clean, white card, and using the same pen, write in your best handwriting, the following:

THIS IS THE PLACE WHERE I REPEAT MY GOALS. REPEATING MY GOALS BRINGS ME CLOSER TO ACHIEVING THEM.

This card is called the 'setting of place' card, put this card aside with your goal card.
You will also need a sheet of clean, white, good quality A4 paper which has not been folded, put this with your two cards and your rough sheet upon which you have written your goals.
You are now ready to begin the first phase.

STEP 3: Setting of Place

Choose a place for your work where you feel comfortable, and are unlikely to be disturbed. The entire program will only take about fifteen minutes every day but remember you may have to say some things out loud and this could be embarrassing.
If you have your own bedroom, then this is ideal; otherwise, choose a time when you are likely to be alone, and select a place (an armchair is sufficient) which you can use for your work.
You will not always be able to do your work in this special place, but you should aim to do so as often as possible.
Now choose two times during the day when you will do this important work. This should be one session in the morning, and one in the afternoon or evening. Two, seven-minute sessions a day is all that is required to make this method bring BIG RESULTS for you.

You will not always be able to do your work at these exact times, but you should aim to as often as possible. You can now start on the practical work!

Here's what you do next:

STEP FOUR:

At your chosen time, go to the chosen place and take out the 'setting of place' card.

STEP FIVE:

Stand, and with your arm extended (as though pointing at something straight ahead of you) inscribe a large capital 'G' in the air in front of you. This 'G' stands for 'Goals' and serves to alert the subconscious mind to what you are about to do.

If you can visualise this 'G' hanging in the air after you have inscribed it, then so much the better.

STEP SIX:

Now sit quietly and relax for about one minute. Try and clear your mind of the confusing thoughts of the day.

Take the 'setting of place' card and read it out loud. Try to feel the 'specialness' of the place where you are working; for the moment, at least, it is dedicated solely to helping you to achieve success.

STEP SEVEN:

Now take the goal card, read it OUT LOUD (if possible), otherwise whisper it under your breath!

IMAGINE yourself getting up at the required time and on the required date to write your goals. 'Hear' the alarm clock going off and 'see' yourself springing out of bed at exactly the time stated. This visualisation is most important.

STEP EIGHT:

When you have done this, stand again, and pointing in the manner described before, un-trace the capital 'G'; that is trace it in reverse so that it 'vanishes'. This tells the subconscious that you have finished the exercise of goal setting.

That's all there is to it......for the moment.

Repeat this exercise twice every day, at your chosen times, and at your chosen place, until the evening before the date you wrote on your goal card. As I said, this should be only a few days away.

On the evening of your big day, set your alarm clock for the time stated (two hours earlier than you normally get up). In the morning, when the alarm rings, spring out of bed. DO NOT DALLY or allow yourself 'another five minutes'. We are playing for BIG stakes here; you're not getting up to go fishing! What you achieve here will allow you to get EVERYTHING YOU HAVE EVER WANTED; don't blow it for the sake of an extra hour or two in bed!

After getting dressed, take the sheet of plain, white A4 paper and a good quality pen (as before). Now copy your goals from your rough sheet of paper onto the sheet of A4. Use your very best and neatest handwriting, and take your time. If you make a mistake, screw up the sheet and start again.

You should end up with your six (or so) goals written neatly, with no mistakes onto one sheet of A4. Fold this sheet in any suitable manner, and place it somewhere for safe keeping. Choose a place where other people will not stumble across it, but where you can get easy access to it yourself.

Don't go back to bed, just use this extra time for whatever you want.

YOU HAVE NOW ACHIEVED YOUR FIRST GOAL! (Getting up at the stated time.)

If, by some accident, you DID NOT manage to get up, then you should regard this as a serious setback. The only remedy is to start again, and MAKE SURE that you get up next time!

Why Go to All This Bother?

The reasons are complex and would take a separate book to explain them thoroughly. Put simply, the purpose of this exercise is to alert the subconscious that you are serious about this business, and to start getting it into the habit of RESPONDING TO YOUR WILL.

Remember I said that the subconscious doesn't like to change? I also said, at that time, "Tough luck!". You will need to show the subconscious that YOU are the master or mistress of your destiny, that YOU are going to start calling the shots from now on and that if YOU decide that you want to change, then the subconscious WILL change in accordance. It won't LIKE it but hard luck!

This little exercise of getting up early is the first step on the way to sharpening your will-power. Believe me, you will need buckets of willpower to succeed.

This exercise has a secondary benefit. It proves to you that the system of goal-setting works! At least for small goals. This is part of the step-by-step approach which I outlined in the opening chapter. By achieving success with small goals, you will come to believe that larger goals can be achieved.

Now onto the important work of realising your first set of goals: Here's how to do it.

Twice a day, at your chosen time, go to your chosen place and proceed as follows:

STEP NINE:

Take out the 'setting of place' card.

Stand, as before, and inscribe the large capital 'G' in the air in front of you. Try to visualise this 'G' hanging in the air after you have inscribed it.

Now sit quietly and relax for about one minute. Try and clear your mind of the hurly-burly thoughts of the day.

Taking the 'setting of place' card read it OUT LOUD (if possible), otherwise whisper it. There is no need to look at the card if you have remembered the words. Once again, feel the 'specialness' of your chosen working place.

Now unfold your sheet of paper upon which you have written your goals. Read each one slowly, out loud (if possible). As you read each goal, IMAGINE it coming true.

For example, if one of the goals is to ask your boss for a rise, then vividly imagine yourself knocking on the office door, going in, asking for a rise, and being granted it.

If one of your later, larger goals is to get £100,000, then strongly visualise your bank statement, SEE the computer entry of £100,000, and note the total on the statement is in excess of this figure. If you have no bank account, then imagine someone giving you bundles of £10 notes. SEE and FEEL the money as it is counted into your hands.

If you have written that you will book a holiday by next Friday, then see yourself going into the travel agent, choosing a holiday, paying for it and walking out with the tickets.

THIS VISUALISATION IS MOST IMPORTANT AND SHOULD NOT BE SKIPPED.

When you have done this, stand again, and pointing in the manner described before, un-trace the capital 'G'; that is trace it in reverse so that it 'vanishes'. This tells the subconscious that you have finished the exercise of goal setting.

Finally, put your various pieces of paper away somewhere out of sight of prying eyes.

Over the next few days, make absolutely sure that you carry out all of the actions you have written in your goals. Fix that shelf, make that call, visit that relative, book that holiday. DO IT.

This is VITAL to your success. Give these tasks absolute priority over everything else which you do. You CAN and WILL achieve these things.

Small Goals – Big Rewards

Why are these relatively small goals so important? Because they represent the first battle between the inertia of your subconscious, and your will power. You MUST win this first skirmish and prove your mastery.

THERE IS NOTHING WHICH YOUR SUBCONSCIOUS MIND WOULD LIKE BETTER THAN TO HAVE YOU FAIL IN ACHIEVING THESE SMALL GOALS!

Why? Because it knows very well what's going on! It knows that once you start achieving these small goals, you will begin work on larger, life-changing, goals; and it doesn't want that!

If it can scupper you at this early stage by making you forget to do your exercises, or ensuring that you simply can't find the time to make that call or do that job, then it has WON. Your deadline dates will pass without you achieving your goals and you will discount my system, then give up. This is exactly what your subconscious wants. You can then go back to blaming everything and everybody for your lack of success. You can even blame me!

This is your first trial by fire. Remember that your enemy is INERTIA. The inertia which tells you that you still have two weeks left to complete your goals....plenty of time. The inertia which tells you to do it tomorrow; after all, you're really *tired* now and you *need* a rest. Inertia makes you skip your exercise period; somehow there just wasn't the *time* was there? Inertia keeps you very, very busy with other 'important' things whilst the precious moments to deadline tick away.

This first battle is the hardest. The way to win it is to make those goals come true sooner, rather than later.

As you achieve each goal, cross it off the list. This is tremendously satisfying! But don't write in any more goals at this stage, until you have achieved them all. This should not take more than a few weeks.

A Word of Warning

It is not a good idea to tell other people what you are doing. In particular, do not let them know your goals.

I don't know why, but it has been my experience that it has a powerful reducing effect upon your progress if other people know what you are attempting to do.

Keep it to yourself for the moment. Don't even share it with your closest partner; unless they want to use the method themselves, and have their own (secret) goals. A little cycnicism from a trusted friend or partner can do a lot of damage at this stage.

By the way, a dire curse descends upon those who lend or borrow this book! Get them to buy their own copy!

Setting Larger Goals

First of all, don't alter the two goals which affect your I-CAN belief. These should always be in place.

After you have achieved your first set of goals, you can progress onto the next level of achievement with some confidence.

For this next level, I suggest that you choose goals from the intermediate level (one of which you should have included in your first list of goals).

Here is a sample of intermediate-level goals; there are obviously thousands of possible goals. (Assume today's date is Jan 1st 1990):-

"By February 20th I will own a new VHS video recorder type JVX 1600PD."

"By March 1st I will have resigned from my job. By this date I will have found a job working as an apprentice vet. This is something I have always wanted to do, I owe it to myself, and I will do it."

"By March 1st I will have turned my £1000 savings into £2000."

"I will spend the next six weekends with my wife and children."

"By April 5th I will have formed my own limited company."

This should give you some idea of the intermediate-level, together with typical time-scales. Notice that the time-scales are much longer (two months, typically), so you will have to be much more patient. But the goals are much bigger, so they are worth waiting longer for!

I have set, and achieved, many such intermediate goals in my life – this is the most common level of goal.

Write these (and all future) goals down on a clean, white sheet of A4, as before, except there is no need to get up two hours early to do it. Repeat them twice a day, in your chosen place and at your chosen time, exactly in the manner described for your simple goals.

As you achieve each goal (and you WILL achieve them if you follow my method) you may cross it off the list and add a new one as and when you like. Make sure that you cross the goals out neatly (use a ruler). I am not being pedantic over this; your goal-sheet is a serious document and you don't want it devalued by scribble and scruffy crossing-out. You wouldn't do that on a legal document, so don't do it on this document.

What Next

When you think that things are going really well for you, and you have achieved quite a few (six at least) intermediate-level goals, then you are ready for the big time. Remember, only a few months will have elapsed since you started using the Midas Method and you are already poised to set yourself some really big goals. These are the exciting ones!

How To Set Really Big Goals

By this stage, your PSI and I-CAN belief levels should both be improving steadily, both through the use of the exercises, (chapters 8, 9 and 10), and through actually achieving your goals. This is the time to start introducing, *gradually* some big-time goals.

These are what I call 'big-time' goals; although you may have your own ideas. (Assume today is Jan 1st 1990):

"By December 31st 1998, my net assets will be in excess of one million pounds."

"By September 1st 1990, I will own a brand-new Porsche 911, red, with leather seats."

"Starting with £100, I will build a limited company which has a turnover of £250,000 by December 31st 1991. This company will be highly profitable."

"I will be married/divorced by August 1st 1991."

"On February 1st 1990 I will give up smoking and never start again."

These are just a few of the thousands of possibilities. You may think them tame, but the chances are that you find them fairly, shall we say, challenging?

Note how I have allowed realistic time-scales to do all these things. I have allowed eight years for you to become a millionaire. That's not too bad is it? What chance do you have of becoming a millionaire without my system?

I have set, and achieved quite a few goals of this 'big-time' size and achieved them all.

The problem you face is setting your goals too small! Yes – too small! When working out your goals, the trick is to put down what you REALLY WANT without worrying about HOW you are going to get it.

If you REALLY WANT a million pounds, then put a million pounds down. Don't put 100,000 because you can't really see how you can get any more than that! That's your poor I-CAN and PSI belief coming through. As I told you earlier, tens of thousands of people are millionaires; there's nothing so special about it and YOU can become one if you want to.

Your goals may genuinely be much more modest; after all, not everyone would thank you for a million pounds. If this is the case, and you genuinely want smaller goals, then that's fine. Just make sure that you are not selling yourself short.

Don't put down a new FORD if you really want a PORSCHE. Don't put down £100,000 pounds if you really want a million. Don't put down a three-bedroom 'semi' if you really want a six-bedroom detached house.

The method of achieving these larger goals is exactly the same as you have been using for the small and intermediate-level goals.

You will need patience, determination and staying power to make these big things happen, but they WILL happen if you believe in yourself enough. Fifteen minutes every day, that's all it takes. Not much is it? Yet it is enough to bring you everything you have ever and will ever want in life, not just material things either, but emotional and spiritual contentment.

That's a big claim, but I guarantee that it works.

BUILDING PSI-BELIEF

10

Liking Yourself

In this chapter I am going to tell you how to build a Positive Self Image using several extremely powerful techniques.

Do you recall how I told you that a Positive Self Image is the first essential step towards success? Think of it as the rock, the foundation upon which your success will be built. Just as you would not attempt to build a house on poor foundations you cannot build success upon a Negative Self Image; if you try to do so, you WILL FAIL, I guarantee it! Just like my friend in the earlier chapter on PSI-belief, life will always seem to conspire mysteriously to ensure your downfall. Of course, there is nothing mysterious about it; you are acting in such a way as to ensure your own failure – you are sabotaging yourself.

The pay-off is SECURITY, you don't have to change any of those large jigsaw-puzzle pieces which make up your World View.

Together we are going to start changing those pieces from 'Failure' pieces to 'Success' pieces.

Changing

Remember the 'corridor of life'? Your lack of PSI-belief keeps dozens of those exciting doors firmly closed and locked, each closed door has a gold-inlaid RESERVED sign upon it. I am going to help you realise that the RESERVED sign means RESERVED FOR YOU, and together we are going to unlock those doors so that you can explore the exciting opportunities which lie behind each one.

In the earlier chapter on PSI-belief, I explained that this part of the subconscious is not influenced by rational argument. If you feel unworthy, no amount of logical, reasoned argument on my part will persuade you otherwise. If this is so, how can we then start to reduce your Negative Self Image? How can we change a NSI into a PSI and thereby unlock the potential to enjoy life to the full? This change can only happen when you *believe* that you *deserve* to enjoy life to the full.

The answer is that you must use the same tools to form your POSITIVE self-image as were used to form your NEGATIVE self image. These tools are FEELING, EMOTION and IMAGINATION, (not reason, logic and rationalisation).

The techniques which I will give you in this chapter may cause problems for some people. Because we are a 'rational' society, we are used to solving all problems with logical, mental processes and we distrust our own feelings and emotions. Men, particularly, are encouraged to treat all emotions with extreme suspicion; women are luckier in this respect.

We think that feelings and emotions are nuisances to be suppressed – wiped out all together if possible. This ludicrous viewpoint has much unhappiness to answer for; the sooner we re-integrate the emotional side of our nature, the happier (and safer) the world will be.

Be that as it may, the ONLY way to tackle your NSI is through the use of these three tools, (feeling, emotion and imagination). After all, that is how it was formed in the first place. It was not the CONTENT of what was said to you as a child which reduced your PSI, but the EMOTIONAL TONE of the exchange.

If your sport's master said kindly to you: "You're not very good at sport, are you Jones?" then your PSI would be unlikely to suffer; however, if the same thing was said with dripping sarcasm and loathing, your PSI would hear the 'hidden message' concealed, (thinly), in the EMOTIONAL TONE. The message your PSI hears is: "I hate you Jones, you're useless at everything." This has the effect of lowering the level of your PSI.

It is for this very reason that you cannot increase your PSI by intellectualisation. It is useless for someone to say to you (or for you to say to yourself), "You're a really worthwhile person," because the CONTENT (although true) will not touch your PSI.

YOUR PSI RESPONDS ONLY TO EMOTIONS, FEELINGS AND IMAGES.

So what *will* work?

Well, for example, a friend could boost your PSI by giving you a warm hug, WITHOUT SAYING A WORD. Your PSI would also be boosted if you met a friend in the street and they gave you a broad smile and said, "I was *really hoping* to meet you today, it's really *great* to see you!" Note that the actual *words* are totally unimportant, it is the EMOTIONAL CONTENT which will boost your PSI, the FEELING that they really *are* glad to see you. If the same words are said insincerely, your PSI (which ignores the words anyway), will detect the sham and be *reduced* because it will hear the 'secret message': "Oh it's you, I really didn't want to meet you, but I suppose I'd better put a brave face on it by pretending to be really pleased to see you."

Think of this part of your subconscious as a filter which rejects words and accepts feelings and emotions.

POSITIVE feelings and emotions directed towards you INCREASE your PSI, whilst NEGATIVE emotions and feelings directed towards you DECREASE your PSI.

Here, then is the secret of increasing your PSI. You must increase the amount of POSITIVE feelings and emotions directed towards you and decrease, (preferably eliminate), NEGATIVE feelings and emotions.

STEP ONE: Eliminating Negative Influences

Fortunately very few of you will need to take any action at all, at this point. I have included this step only for people who are, *even now* , being subjected to a daily barrage of negative feelings and emotions.

Most of us left school a long time ago, (school can be a major source of negative strokes) and, if you had an unhappy childhood, hopefully that is behind you as well. The majority of people are not exposed to many negative strokes during the course of a week; although we all get some occasionally. However, some people *are* in a situation where they receive a high rate of negative strokes. These people receive more negative strokes in a day, than you or I receive in a month of normal life. They are obviously very unhappy people.

It is my experience that nearly all of these people fall into two categories:

1. Those still living at home with parents.
2. Those trapped in a bad marriage or relationship.

Of the two categories, number two represents by far the largest category of unhappy people.

There are many other smaller groups of people, (for example, people in the armed services who find themselves bullied), but these represent a small fraction of the total – nevertheless this rule applies to them also.

You must be involved intimately, on a day-to-day basis with other people, before you can suffer from an excess of negative strokes.

Bad marriages and relationships are PERFECT for this! They offer endless scope for two people to batter away at each other's PSI until they are reduced to zero. In practice, the PSI of either partner never quite reaches zero because a defensive wall is built up to prevent fatal damage. This wall eventually stops the partners from even talking to each other, it is an essential defence mechanism.

It is impossible to build up your PSI much above zero if you are trapped in one of these unhappy situations. It is like poking your head cautiously above a wall only to have it shot off!

The Solution

IF, DESPITE YOUR BEST EFFORTS AT RECONCILIATION WITH YOUR INTIMATE ASSOCIATE(S), YOU ARE STILL TRAPPED IN A DEEPLY UNHAPPY RELATIONSHIP, THEN GET OUT, WHATEVER THE COST.

I am not an 'agony uncle' and I am not setting myself up as a marriage guidance counselor; I am looking at this from one viewpoint only:- If you want to be happy and successful, you must first remove yourself from any source of negative strokes.

Even the powerful techniques which I am giving you in this book will not be proof against a continual barrage of negative feelings and emotions – DON'T EVEN TRY THEM, you'll be wasting your time.

If, despite everything, you decide to remain in your unhappy situation, then fine. For your own reasons you will have chosen an unhappy, unfulfilling life for yourself and you will have turned your back on personal success; that is your choice, but there is no point in reading further, this book is not for you.

Most people who are in an unhappy relationship remain there for one of two reasons. Either they believe it is 'better' that way, or they simply cannot see a way out. In either case they are almost always mistaken. One unhappy person in a relationship quickly makes for two unhappy people; why should two people stay together and make each other unhappy? I have never been given a convincing reason. "The children," is the reason most often given, even though the unhappy relationship is making the children unhappy too!

Anyone who has been through the trauma of a divorce or split with children involved, knows afterwards that it is the best thing they ever did, even though it was intensely painful at the time.

I have restricted my comments to relationships, but the same rule applies if you find yourself in any situation where you are subjected to continual negative strokes – try your hardest to put it right, and if it still won't work, then get out.

If you ARE in an unhappy relationship, and have decided to get out but cannot see a way; then this book can definitely help you. When you have read the chapter on goal-setting, you will know how to set a date by which you will have removed yourself into happier circumstances. Once you have done this, you can start to improve your PSI level, but not before.

This book can also help you to improve your relationship with your intimate associates, by setting goals and visualising a more harmonious interaction.

As I said, this step probably will not apply to you, if that is the case then move straight on to:

STEP TWO: Good Morning!

I'll tell you how to boost your PSI:- Just go out and get lots of people to really love you and to be warm, loving and kind to you every single day!

If only it were that simple, your PSI would be miraculously increased within a very short period of time. Unfortunately it seems hard to find so many willing volunteers! In fact you have probably noticed a strange quirk of human nature which works as follows:

The more you 'ask' other people (either verbally or non-verbally) for affection, warmth and love, the less they will give.

The converse is also true: **Those people who don't seem to need warmth, love and affection, and never ask for it, are those people who seem to get the most!** Strange isn't it?

This situation doesn't occur if you *occasionally* 'ask' for love, for example if you just feel a bit down one day. Most people will respond with warmth; the problem occurs if you *keep on* asking for it on a regular basis.

So, if we cannot find an army of slaves to pat us on the back each day, what *can* we do?

The answer is we pat OURSELVES on the back! Metaphorically, that is.

The Method:

Every morning, when you get up and go to the bathroom, look at yourself in the mirror, smile broadly at yourself and say (out loud if possible), "Good morning, you're looking really great today!"

Then FEEL warm thoughts towards yourself, feel as much love as possible, put real emotion behind this.

DON'T look in the mirror and think things like: "God I look old!", or "I'm really ugly." This is a really bad habit to get into – break it now.

Like most of the steps in this book, this step may seem deceptively simple. You may even find this particular step amusing; but I am very serious indeed. This step, like ALL the steps, has been carefully worked out and tested over many years and found to be truly effective in raising your PSI.

When you first try it, you will undoubtedly feel a little strange, if not foolish; after all, you are not used to talking to yourself – but that is going to change. You will be doing a lot of talking to yourself from now on.

This step is the second of four powerful exercises which I will give to you to help you to get into a dialogue with your subconscious. By 'dialogue' I do not mean intellectual sentences and phrases; I am talking about an EMOTIONAL DIALOGUE, for this is the only sort of dialogue which will affect your PSI.

When you give yourself this "good morning" greeting, you are starting to build up a bond of trust between your conscious and subconscious minds. You are giving yourself positive strokes, thereby boosting your PSI; you are unraveling the evil spell of the past.

How long will it take before it starts to work?

When I started to use this technique, it still felt strange after two weeks, thereafter it started to seem quite natural and I actually felt my PSI being gradually enhanced. I could notice a definite benefit after only one month.

Start using this technique first thing tomorrow. Promise yourself that you will use it for at least a month, I guarantee that you will notice a change in that time.

STEP THREE: Treat Yourself!

Are you one of those people who rarely, if ever, treat themselves to anything? Well now is the time to start changing that!

If you often treat yourself because you feel that you deserve it, then great! You can skip this step and move onto the next one.

Our society teaches us to believe that it is selfish to buy things for ourselves just because we feel we deserve them. We feel positively GUILTY about sneaking into a shop and buying ourselves a present. Often we cover this guilt by purchasing presents for about six other people at the same time! This is very expensive and unnecessary!

People who never treat themselves often hide behind a mask of 'goodness'; they are always buying little presents or preparing surprises for *other* people, but never themselves. In fact, it is difficult to give a present to a person like this; they will try very hard not to accept it, positively wallowing in modesty and humility!

Why do they do this? Simple! Their lack of PSI means that they don't think that they are *worth* treating; they believe that almost anyone else in the world deserves a treat more than they do. The little gifts and surprises which they give to other people are really the things which they would like to give to themselves. By giving them to other people, they can earn little pats on the back for being a "terribly kind and thoughtful person."

I know someone who spends nearly all of her spare time doing things for other people. She is always popping round to one of her large circle of friends to see if there are any little favours which she can do. She never, ever forgets a birthday and you only have to mention, in passing, that you like a certain thing, and it will turn up a short while later, tastefully gift-wrapped.

The interesting point is that she never does anything for herself because she is too busy doing things for other people! She hardly ever goes out for an evening's entertainment, rarely takes a holiday or buys new clothes. She prefers to spend her money on other people, in fact she puts everyone else in front of herself. The result is that people like her superficially, but they do not respect her; they class her as "nice, but harmless". This is a wishy-washy statement to have made about you.

It is a true fact that people **genuinely like, admire and respect those people who like, admire and respect themselves.**

I am not advocating long-term selfishness. It is always good to do whatever you can for people, and genuine kindness and thoughtfulness are qualities to be admired. I am talking here about an almost obsessive degree of selflessness, based, not on genuine altruism, but on a Negative Self Image.

You can greatly increase your PSI level by spending more time, effort and money on *yourself* rather than other people. The one and only excuse you need for doing this is that you *deserve it* . If you think that this sounds selfish then fine! I want you to BE selfish for as long as it takes to raise your PSI to a point where you KNOW that you are a really worth-while person. When you get to this point, *then* is the time to decide what is selfish and what is not, and to moderate your behaviour accordingly.

Buy that new dress or shirt you have wanted. Take that holiday. Go out, have fun, enjoy yourself. Above all, treat yourself to TIME. Time to be by yourself if you want to, time to go out shopping (for you), time to read that book. Don't be a servant to other people, they are just as capable as you of looking after themselves. If you have children , don't run round after them and pander to their every whim; spend *less* time being a skivvy and *more* time being a real human being.

People won't like it at first, but I can guarantee that they will soon get used to it and start respecting you a great deal more, when you start respecting yourself.

You don't need to make any excuses about indulging yourself; all you need to say is that you felt that you *deserved* it.

From now on, you are going to start loving yourself a lot more; you are going to start looking after yourself and putting yourself FIRST occasionally, not always LAST.

DON'T BE SURPRISED IF PEOPLE WIPE THEIR FEET ON YOU IF YOU ARE DOING A VERY GOOD IMPRESSION OF A DOORMAT!

If you still think that all this sounds very selfish, then let me tell you that being kind to yourself like this, will have a *positive* effect on the people around you, not a *negative effect*. Why? Because if *you* are happy and well-adjusted, then this reflects onto those people in your intimate contact, and they become happier also – even if you are doing less for them than before.

When you start being kind to yourself, the subconscious responds almost immediately. After a very short while, it starts to believe in its own self-worth, your PSI is enhanced. After all, if you are treating yourself to all these things, you MUST be a worthwhile person; only people who feel worthless go around acting as though everyone else's wishes and desires were always more important than their own.

The only exception to this rule is if you GENUINELY believe that you want to spend your life helping other people and that you want to sacrifice your own life to the common good. If this is *really true* then you must already love yourself completely, because anyone who attempts altruism without first loving themselves is doomed to failure. If this is you, then why are you reading this book???!!!

STEP FOUR: Think Kind Thoughts About Yourself

This is a useful technique because it can be performed anywhere, at any time you have an odd moment to spare. Here is what you do:

Using any spare moments which you have, mentally greet your subconscious in rather the same spirit as in your 'morning mirror' exercise. Now send kind, loving, supportive thoughts out to your subconscious; remember it is the FEELING behind these thoughts which is important rather than the actual words.

This is a difficult exercise to describe because it is to do with feelings, but you should aim towards a feeling of harmonious comradeship with your subconscious. Your EMOTIONAL TONE should be the same as you would have towards a much loved brother or sister. The thought should be: "You and me....we're a team...we're going places!"

I do this exercise whilst driving along in the car; it only takes a minute or so and I always make myself feel better with it.

Done properly and often, this exercise can bring big dividends.

Mr. VIP

I once had a friend who was terribly shy. He had a real problem with meeting new people, and, at parties, he was always found in the kitchen helping with the washing-up. This friend had the lowest Positive Self Image that I have ever come across; he genuinely believed that most other people were superior to him and were secretly sneering at him. In truth, he was a likable person with plenty to offer.

One day he asked for my help. His shyness was causing severe depression, and he was almost living the life of a hermit in an attempt to avoid people. I thought for a long while, then suggested the following solution:

I suggested that, no matter how bad he felt inside, he should *act* as though he was a VIP. I told him that I wasn't asking him to change in any way, but merely to *act* as though a change had taken place. I asked him to imagine that he was an actor playing the part of an extremely important person; we would both know that he was acting, but that didn't matter.

Fortunately my friend had a reasonable amount of money (he never went out, remember) and so I told him to go out and buy a complete set of new clothes – the sort the character he was playing would wear. His existing clothes and dress sense were truly frightful, but obviously I didn't tell him this. I also told him to go to the sort of places that his character would frequent. Instead of the local sleazy pub which he drank in occasionally, I suggested the name of a few really up-market (and expensive) bars. I also took the liberty of booking us both into a very expensive restaurant at the end of the week.

I suggested that the experiment would last for one week, during which he would act as much as possible like the character he was playing. He agreed, and even took a week off work for the experiment.

The results were truly astounding! After only five days we met up, in the restaurant, and I had trouble recognising him! The outfit he had purchased must have cost hundreds, but it made him look like he was worth millions! I felt shabby in comparison! The waiter approached us, and immediately assumed that my friend was the important person and that I was his guest; he fussed around him and paid scant attention to me!

When we had settled down, my friend excitedly told me about his week. He had been to an expensive night-club and drank high-priced cocktails all evening. At the night-club he was asked to join in with a group of people for the evening. These were the sort of people who wouldn't have given him the time of day the week before. He had invented some story about being the director of a building company, and more than managed to hold his own with the other people at the table.

Later in the week he had traveled to London to see the sights – first class. A taxi had taken him everywhere he wanted to go; and he even had afternoon tea at the Dorchester Hotel! He ended up the evening by seeing a top musical ('Cats') on a Saturday night! How did he get the ticket? From a ticket-tout at the stage-door – fifty pounds a seat! He didn't care; he figured that the character he was playing would not have worried about the expense – so my friend didn't!

In short, he was a transformed person. He had received so many positive strokes from people in the space of one short week that he realised that he must have been doing something wrong before, after all, he was exactly the same person.

He realised that merely by *acting* as though he was a worthwhile person ensured that *other people* TREATED him like a worthwhile person, whereas acting like a nobody ensured that everyone TREATED him like a nobody!

There is a very great lesson for us all to learn here, that is why I want you to start treating yourself like royalty. You may not be able to afford the kind of extravagant week that my friend had (he told me later that it cost him over 1000!), but you do not need to go to such great lengths to prove to yourself that people treat you exactly how you expect them to treat you, no more, no less.

Why not try my friend's experiment for yourself? Spend one week (that's not really a lot, is it?) treating yourself like a VIP and see the startling effect that it has on your PSI. I will guarantee that it will shoot up!

By the way, my friend is a permanently changed person. He liked playing a VIP so much that he has taken over the part full-time! After some initial shock from his close friends and associates, they now all treat him like he was the boss! The more they do this, the more he *feels like* he is the boss. This is what happens if you boost your PSI by using this method.

In this chapter I have divulged some powerful methods of improving your PSI. Remember that it is *essential* to have a Positive Self Image before you can succeed. You will definitely fail without a strong PSI.

Don't be tempted to dismiss these exercises as "silly," or "a waste of time." Believe me, they work – thousands of people have proved it beyond doubt. All I ask you to do is TRY. If you just TRY then you will know for yourself.

SUMMARY OF TECHNIQUES

11

You're on the way! I have now told you everything that you need to know in order to succeed. I haven't held anything back, and the method which I have shared with you in this book is exactly the method which brought me my present-day success. Tens of thousands of people have used techniques like this to bring big results in their personal lives; there is nothing new about Positive Thinking and Visualisation – successful people have been using it either consciously or unconsciously for thousands of years to get exactly what they want.

The single biggest obstacle in your path at the moment, is your INERTIA. It is up to you to choose – right now – whether you are going to bumble through life hoping for the best, or take firm control of your destiny and start achieving everything you could possibly wish for, or dream of. All you have to do is try my method; it's that simple – just TRY.

It is an amazing fact that quite a large number of people reading this book will not even bother to TRY the system, not even once! They will read this book through from cover to cover, as though it were a novel; decide that the ideas sound really promising, then do *absolutely nothing at all about it!* The book will get put on one side and forgotten. I don't want that to happen to you, I want you to succeed and to have all the things which you deserve.

The Sky's the Limit

What sort of things could you achieve using these techniques? The answer – in case you haven't already guessed – is ANYTHING!

Here are just a few of the things which you could do (in order of difficulty). I have listed these in order to stimulate your imagination, but hopefully you are already starting to dream up your own list.

You could:-

Make a million pounds.
Give up work completely.
Get the house you really want.

Get the car you really want.
Buy a boat or holiday home.
Eat in expensive restaurants.
Wear the best clothes.
Pay yourself any salary you want to.
Buy yourself time to do the things you REALLY want to do.
Write a novel/play/music/poetry.
Learn something new (languages, musical instrument, driving, flying etc).
Change your job. Do something you REALLY want to do.
Take as much holiday as you want.
Visit any foreign country you want.
Start your own business.
Have time for your hobbies and interests.
Have happy relationships with people.
Allow yourself quiet time to meditate, philosophise or just think.
Start to be calm, content, and truly happy.
Start to remove all of your negative character traits.
Improve your positive character traits.
Have people like, admire and respect you.
Have no enemies, only friends.

This is quite a long and impressive list isn't it? Yet you can achieve any of the things on this list using only the methods given in this book. I KNOW this because I have achieved ALL of the things on this list and many more besides. Yes, that's right, I have achieved EVERY SINGLE THING on the list using only the Midas method. If it can work for me, then it can work for you to.

Summary of Techniques

This chapter summarises all of the various techniques given in this book, and allows you to see, at a glance, the total extent of the exercises which you should carry out.

The work should only take approximately fifteen minutes every day, done in two sessions, one morning and the other afternoon/evening.

I-CAN Belief (Chapter eight)

1. Watch your language! Never say "I can't do that."
2. Never blame anything or anybody else for your misfortune.
3. Grab every opportunity that's going.
4. Set yourself the two I-CAN goals:

   "I can achieve anything I want, the whole world of opportunity is open to me."
   "Every day I am becoming more positive. I am eliminating negative thoughts and feelings."

5. Use goal-setting to tackle particular I-CAN'Ts.

Goal-Setting (Chapter nine)

1. Write simple goals to start with.
2. Write personal improvement goals as though they were actually happening.
3. Write material goals in precise detail, and set a deadline by which they will be accomplished.
4. Write your 'goal-card'. (Getting up two hours earlier.)
5. Write your 'setting of place' card.

Twice daily at your chosen place:

6. Inscribe 'G' in the air.
7. Sit quietly.
8. Recite 'setting of place' formula.
9. Read your 'goal-card' out loud, visualise yourself getting up at the correct time.
10. Un-trace 'G'.
11. Get up early and write your goals neatly.

Achieving all other goals, twice daily at your chosen place:

12. Inscribe 'G' in the air.
13. Sit quietly.
14. Recite 'setting of place' card.
15. Recite your goals and visualise them coming true.
16. Un-trace the 'G'.

PSI-BELIEF (Chapter ten)

1. 'Good morning' exercise. To be performed every day.
2. Put yourself in a positive environment.
3. Treat yourself.
4. Send kind thoughts to yourself. To be performed at odd moments.

If you give yourself a chance, like I did, and suspend your disbelief for a few months, then the results will be truly startling. Just TRY the method for a while. Don't try and rationalise it or worry about HOW it could possibly work, just TRY. You have a huge amount to gain and almost nothing to lose. With those odds, only a fool would spend too much time worrying about HOW the system worked!

GETTING THERE!

It is an amazing fact that quite a large number of people reading this book will not even bother to TRY the system, not even once! They will read this book through from cover to cover, as though it were a novel; decide that the ideas sound really promising, then do *absolutely nothing at all about it!* The book will get put on one side and forgotten about. I don't want that to happen to you, I want you to succeed and to have all the things which you deserve.

Right at the very beginning of this book, I explained that I was not offering a practical business plan, scheme or money-making idea. Believe me, what you have read in these pages is far more valuable than a hundred of these ideas. Using the powerful exercises which I have divulged in this book, WILL bring you three quarters of the way to success.

But what about the last quarter? You may remember that 'getting there' represented the last twenty-five percent of the battle. How can I help you to achieve this?

My difficulty is this:- Whereas the method for achieving the first seventy-five percent is common to all people, the actual practical mechanics of achieving your desires (the last twenty-five percent) varies greatly from person to person.

One aspirant may want to make a million pounds, another only one hundred thousand pounds; the techniques for acquiring these different sums are dissimilar. Someone else might not want money at all, but instead they may wish to play the violin to concert standard, or become a great athlete.

To the person interested in making money, the ideal 'getting there' chapter would be chock-full of good business ideas and tips on running a company. To the athlete, this chapter would contain advice about exercise, diet and where to buy good running shoes. The violin player would need this chapter to contain anecdotes from great musicians, hints on bowing technique, exercise plans and a section on how to spot a bargain in the fiddle world.

Do you see my dilemma? Actually I regard this chapter as the least important in the book. Why? Because if you apply my method properly, a unique, individual opportunity WILL open up for you. My method opens doors in the corridor of life; unlocking those doors is the tricky part of the exercise, walking through them takes only a little effort. I can't tell you *exactly* what opportunities will occur for you, I only know that they WILL occur if you try my method.

With this in mind, I have limited this chapter to passing on the benefit of my experience in the world of money-making. I am sure that this will be of interest to most readers because the possibility of making money probably attracted you to this book in the first place. Money also allows you to realise a lot of non-money related dreams. For example, if you want to be a concert pianist, money can release you from the need to work for a living, thereby giving you the necessary time to practice.

My Background

For the last fifteen years I have been involved in making money. I have done everything from running a small company out of my house, to being the director of a company with a six-figure turnover. During my time in business, I have accumulated quite a lot of experience which I am happy to pass on to you.

If you want to make money, the following tips should prove useful to you:-

How Long?

First of all, the length of time it will take you to make your money depends upon how high a target you have set yourself.

You have to be realistic about this. It is very hard (I have, of course, removed the word "impossible" from my vocabulary, otherwise I might be tempted to use it here) to make a million pounds in six months. However, it is not hard to make, say, fifty thousand pounds in six months.

I don't want to limit your ceiling artificially, but my experience tells me that it will take between five and ten years to make a million pounds. If you think that's a long time, then add up how much you will make over the next ten years if you *don't* go for the million! It's a depressingly small figure.

I made my million in eight years, and even now, most of it is tied up in company shares. It will be about three more years before I can honestly say that I have a million pounds "in the bank," at the moment, my net assets are in excess of a million pounds.

If your aims are more modest, say to make one hundred thousand pounds, then this is quite easy to do in, say, two years (depending upon the amount of money you start out with, and your level of business experience). I could make this amount in just over a year, but then I've been doing it for longer than you.

Again, if two years sounds like a long time to get one hundred thousand pounds, remember, that's over eight thousand pounds a month! How much are you getting every month at the moment?

If your target is to double the value of your house, then this should be possible in a year or two. A brand new Porsche should take six months to a year, a second car should take three to six months. A raise or change of job should take less than three months.

Remember that these are MY ideas of time-scales, based on my experience.

You may be able to do it more quickly than me.

Making a Million

I have to ask you, first of all, do you really want a million pounds? Earlier in the book I said that it was important for you to set your goals high, and not to artificially lower them because of your lack of belief in your own ability. It is also important not to set them higher than they need to be, just for the sake of it. If you would be perfectly happy with a quarter of a million pounds, then don't tie yourself into the heartache and stress of going for a million because if you don't really want it, you won't have the staying power to get it.

This applies to all of your goals. You must be very, very serious about really wanting the things you set out as goals, otherwise you won't have what it takes when the going gets a bit tough.

If you really DO want a million pounds then you can get it. There are many ways of making a million pounds, quite a few of them are illegal! Of the legal options, by far and away the best bet for someone starting from the bottom is to build up a company and then sell it. This is effectively what I did.

There is no hard and fast rule over this, but it will take you at least five years to build a company worth a million pounds and a further three years before you can take the money and run.

It takes three years to get out because a potential buyer of your company sees you, (quite rightly), as a key figure in the success of that company; they will therefore want you to stay on in some capacity until they can assure themselves of the company's prosperity in your absence.

Of course, during a lot of the working life of your company, you will be drawing a nice, big salary cheque, driving a company car, and picking up a lot of other fringe benefits, so you don't have to wait right until the end to get the rewards.

Starting Out

I started my first company from my kitchen table. I had no capital at all and I knew absolutely nothing about running a business, keeping books, accountancy or anything much at all. I WAS good at electronics, and that strength is what I used as a foundation for the business. (What are YOU good at?)

I then worked very, very hard. For five years I worked a seven day week, often twelve hours a day. I lived and breathed my business, and most other things went by the wayside. I didn't mind because I knew that I wanted to 'retire' at thirty-five. By retire, I mean that I wanted to be free from the necessity of *having* to work. I wanted to choose whether I worked or not; if I didn't feel like it, then I wouldn't. I mentioned earlier that I have achieved this goal.

The other thing I did was to take risks. If you don't gamble in life, then you don't ever win! I gambled my house on my ability to succeed. Throughout those five years, the bank were hovering in the background just waiting to snatch my house if I put a foot wrong; believe me, that concentrates the mind wonderfully!

If you are playing for really big stakes, (and a million pounds is big by any standards), then be prepared to work hard and take risks. You can achieve the first seventy-five percent of the success formula from your armchair, but now is the time to get out of it – in fact sell it, because you won't be needing it for a few years!

A lot of people expect big rewards without taking any risks at all! I remember talking recently to a man who genuinely wanted to be rich, but when I explained to him that he would have to take risks in order to achieve this, his face fell. He explained that he was married with three children and that he couldn't possibly put his house on the line, it wouldn't be fair to his family. I had to explain to him that unless his family was behind him all the way, then it would be very hard for him to succeed anyway (remember that one of the first steps to success is to put yourself in an environment where people support your endeavours).

I also pointed out that he had absolutely no guarantee that he wouldn't lose his house tomorrow anyway! With jobs in short supply, he could easily find himself out of work and having his house re-possessed; just like thousands of other people before him.

You CANNOT achieve without some risk. Think of any of the pioneers of the past. Nothing would ever have been achieved if those people had not been prepared to risk a very great deal, sometimes even their lives. You may not be prepared to risk your life in a solo flight across the Atlantic, or an un-supported expedition to the North Pole, but if you want a million pounds you must surely be prepared to risk the very small chance that you might have to sell up and move to a smaller house. It's hardly laying your life on the line is it?

If you want a nice, comfortable, ordinary, un-exciting life then you are quite free to choose that for yourself and your family, but if you are seeking BIG results from life, then be prepared to gamble, to dare and to win. You can drive all of your life in the slow lane and STILL risk running into the back of a parked lorry; or you can pull out into the fast lane occasionally and start experiencing the thrill of high speed motoring!

Above all, don't use your family as an I-CAN'T excuse. You may have a strong desire to hitch up a horse to a Gypsy caravan and go around Europe for a year, but you don't because you fear the disruption to your children's education. But let me ask you this: Would your children be better, more rounded and interesting individuals for this experience? The answer (legal schooling requirements aside for the moment) is undoubtedly YES!

But back to the subject of that elusive million pounds. In order to get it, you will have to (temporarily) give up a lot of other things. You will have to work twice as hard as your friends and colleagues driving in the nice, safe, slow lane, and you will have to take many risks, big and small. Is the reward worth it? Only you can answer this question. I thought that it was worth it, because now I am free to do exactly what I want to do with most of my time. Had I not decided to go for this goal, I would be forced to spend the next twenty-five years working eight hours a day for someone else's benefit. I wasn't prepared to give up my life so readily, after all, forty hours a week was the Lion's share of my active life! Why should I give my life away to make someone else rich? It seems stupid if you ask that simple question, doesn't it? But that is what most of us are doing!

Think about your job for the moment. How important is it *really* ? You may be one of the few people with a genuinely important job (doctor, farmer, nurse, teacher, builder, clothing manufacturer etc) in which case you should consider carefully before giving it up; however MOST people in this country do very unimportant and often even harmful jobs. Try and cut through the ego surrounding your own job and look at the reality. Everyone likes to think that they are important people working in a worthwhile profession, but often this is a justification which keeps you sane, and allows you to carry on! What are you *really* doing with your life? How important is your job?

If, like me, you are waking up to the reality of the illusion which has mesmerized you since birth, and are starting to realise that you DON'T have to have a job, and that you are FREE to spend your life creatively fulfilling yourself as a *person* , then you are on your way to a deeply satisfying life without artificial limits. Making a million may be the way you choose to finally free yourself from this yoke.

Starting a Company

Whether you are after a million, or just a few hundred thousand, the best vehicle for achieving this is via a limited company.

Contrary to popular belief, it is about the easiest thing in the world to become the director of your very own limited company. You don't need qualifications, references or experience to control a company, in fact all you need is about a hundred pounds.

If you look at the "Business Opportunities" section of a paper like 'Exchange and Mart', you will see dozens of adverts offering to sell you "off the shelf" or "made to measure" companies. All you have to do is to choose one of the adverts and send off for details.

In due course you will be sent a list of names of "off the shelf" companies from which to choose. These companies have never traded, and are formed solely with the intention of selling them on to people like yourself.

They will have truly awful names like "Conegate", "Spinbrand", "Sandbook" and other unevocative epithets. The names are awful because they are usually computer-generated by randomly pairing four or five letter words together, however, you might find something you like from the list. If you do, then just send off your cheque, fill in the forms, and within a week you will be the director of your very own company – it's that simple. If you don't like the names on the list, then you can make up your own name. You don't usually pay any extra for this, but it takes about six weeks to get your new name registered. If you buy an "off the shelf" company, you can always change the name later upon payment of a small fee.

Be warned: Almost ANY name you think up will have been used before, so you won't be able to use it! It is quite staggering how many companies there

119

are. I had to try about twenty names before I found one that hadn't been used. The more obvious your name is, the less likely it is to be 'going spare'. For example, if you want to be in publishing, don't even bother with obvious names like "Bookworm", "Muse", "Newscript", or "Page publishing". You will have to choose something very unusual like "Countdown Publishing" or "Nevermore Publishing".

The more words you have in the title, the less likely it is to have been used already. For example, the prior existence of "Countdown Ltd" should not affect your chances of getting the name "Countdown Bible Publishing Ltd".

There are certain restrictions on names, though. For example, you should not imply that you are larger than you really are, or international (if you're not). An example of this is attempting to call your one man saw-sharpening business, "Global Metal Polishing Services International Ltd."

Also to be avoided are titles implying Royal patronage, e.g. "Her Majesty's Saw Sharpening Company Ltd." and titles which will provoke immediate law suites like "Harrods Mail Order Ltd" if your name happens to be Mrs. Harrod.

Apart from these, and one or two other, minor restrictions, the whole field of names is open to you. However, here's a small tip: If you are not exactly sure what you are going to use your company for, or you want to try a few ideas (in different fields) before finally settling on one business plan, then keep the name of your company suitably general. Even though it's awful, at least a name like "Vinewell Ltd" doesn't particularly suggest any field of activity, (unless perhaps underground wine-making?).

Don't saddle yourself with a name like "Processor Data Systems Ltd" if there is a possibility that you might end up wholesaling kippers!

Company Secretary

Ideally you need two people on the board of your company. (You don't need a board-room, by the way, the kitchen table is fine for the moment.) There should be at least one director and a company secretary. The company secretary (not related to a secretary you might find in an office), has certain legal obligations and duties. These are not particularly arduous, but you might like to pass the whole thing on to the company who's advertisement you originally replied to. For an annual fee (about £35 at the time of writing), they will take the whole irritating business off your hands, and act as company secretary on your behalf.

For a similar piffling fee, they will also offer you the use of their address as your company's registered office. Every company must have a registered office in order that the long arm of the law can track you down if you're naughty. If your address happens to be "Flat 6, 14b, Cherry Tree Close", then you might find this address a bit embarrassing on your note-paper – not quite the right image somehow! However, a smart, central-London address as the registered office looks pretty good. You can't use the address as an accommodation address though, so you will have to put your actual address on the note-paper as well, or you could employ the services of an accommodation agency if your own address is really terrible.

An accommodation agency is simply an office with a smart address. For an annual fee, they will let you use their office as your own address, and will forward all mail to your real address. It has to be said that accommodation addresses are usually used by people with something to hide.

Legal Things

Running a limited company provides you with certain benefits and also lands you with certain responsibilities.

You have a legal duty to maintain accurate records of the company's board meetings and decisions taken therein. Also you must submit an annual return to companies house.

A annual return is simply a statement of the balance sheet and profit and loss sheet detailing the company's business over the previous year. These statements are held at companies house and may be viewed by anyone who cares to look at them. This means you too. You are quite free to examine the trading record of any company which is registered there.

Unfortunately, you can't submit the returns yourself. It's not that they don't trust you, but.....! You must get an accountant to submit the returns for you, and this means paying the accountant a fee for this service. However, the fee is most unlikely to be very high if your turnover and profits are reasonable. Be prepared for some steep fees as the money starts to roll in though!

By the way, if your company doesn't trade at all, you can send in a 'zero return' without employing the services of an accountant.

It will be a year or so before you have to submit your first accounts, and they do allow you quite a bit of grace, however, eventually you will have to cough up the figures and this is likely to work to your disadvantage. Your first year's figures are not likely to be earth-shattering, unless you really HAVE found a 'Get Rich Quick' scheme, in which case can you let me know about it?

Once you have sent in the figures, any Tom, Dick or Credit Agency can check you out and spot immediately the size of company you are. This will only cause you a problem if you have lied to your customers about the size of your operation in order to get their business (and, of course, no-one has *ever* done that before), or, you are trying to get credit over and above the level which you can easily support. Anyway, there's not much you can do about it except to bluff your way through the first couple of years like every other company has since history began!

The advantage of being a limited company is that if the company goes broke, the liabilities are restricted to the assets of the company. In short, they can take your typewriter, but not your house.

The Sting

There is a catch though. Unless you are very well off and can fund your company from day one and into the future, then at some stage you will need to borrow money for the growth of the company. If you are running the business correctly, then your bank manager will probably be prepared to consider lending you a modest sum; BUT (and here is the catch) you won't get a penny unless the borrowing is secured against some tangible asset – like your house. So guess what? If the company goes bust, you lose your house (or at least that part which was secured against the loan!) – scratch the major benefit of being limited!

You may be tempted to ask why you should be a limited company. The answer is that a limited company is the only acceptable vehicle for a *serious* business person. If you want to dabble around a bit or do a spot of painting and decorating on the side, then don't bother with a limited company, just trade under your own name.

VAT

If you think that your *turnover* is likely to exceed about 22,000 a year (at the time of writing) then you must register for VAT. This has advantages for you, as you can claim back all the VAT which you pay out on the items which the company buys, including capital items like typewriters and telephone answering machines.

VAT returns are really simple to keep and should not cause you any problems.

What Next?

So let us assume that you are now the director of your own company. What is the next step?

Firstly you will need a bank account. If you already have a private account then go and see your bank manager and talk over the opening of a business account at the same branch. You should have prepared a business plan and have sent him or her a copy in advance.

What is a business plan? Important, that's what it is! A business plan is a professionally presented, (typed) document prepared by yourself, which outlines the business you are proposing to undertake. It need not be more than ten pages long, but should explain clearly, in plain English, the following points:

1. The type of business in which you are proposing to engage: (E.g. window cleaning services).
2. The market for your goods and services: (E.g. 10,000 windows within a short walk of your home).
3. The competition: (There are only two other window cleaners in the whole area, and one of them is ninety-five years old.)
4. The market penetration: You expect to be able to get ten percent of the windows onto your books within six months, that's one thousand windows. Back this up with facts, for example actually go and ASK one

hundred people if you can clean their windows for them, and make sure that at least ten percent say "yes".

5. Servicing the market: Give figures and times to prove that you can actually clean one thousand windows a week using your available resources.
6. Business overheads: Note down the cost of buckets, a bicycle, ladders, leathers, soap, squeegee, insurance, leaflets, telephone, etc. Make sure that you've thought of everything.
7. Cash flow forecast: This is the most important page, and probably the only one which your bank manager will read:-

Cash-flow Forecast

The Cash Flow Forecast shows, month by month, how the business will progress, cash-wise. It is only your best guess at this stage, but your bank manager will judge your seriousness and fitness for business by the amount of insight which you show in preparing this forecast.

If you can't find someone to help you in preparing a cash flow forecast, then most books on running a small business will have a section on preparing these forecasts.

In simple terms, you divide a sheet of paper into twelve columns, each column is labeled with a month, starting with the first month of the forecast. In the first row, you put the number of sales which you expect to achieve in each month. You are not likely to get all of your customers in the first week of trading, but rather as your reputation increases, the number of customers will increase. The bank manager will be looking for a gradually rising level of sales, as this shows a realistic approach.

If your eventual target is four thousand windows a month, then your first month's sales might be one thousand, (two hundred and fifty a week) building to four thousand over a six month period.

In the next row, put the value of those sales in pounds. If you are planning to charge one pound per window, then this row will have the same figures as the row above. The next few rows are used to show your overheads and materials. For example, each window might use ten pence worth of soap and other materials, this row will then show ten pence for every window 'sold' in the sales row. Your telephone bill will be shown as four quarterly payments going out in month one, four, eight and twelve. Put all your overheads and expenses down in this manner, using as many separate rows as you need.

Don't forget a row for your drawings (wages). How much are you going to take from the business every month?

After you have completed this exercise, the bottom row should be used to total the monthly columns. The totals are given by subtracting from the monthly sales, all the other amounts in that column.

Having completed this, anyone can see, at a glance, how the company will fare over the coming months. Just looking along the bottom row will tell you immediately the maximum amount of money which will need to be borrowed (if at all). Needless to say, the bottom row should show a gradually rising monthly profit.

If you prepare your business plan carefully, then your bank manager will be inclined to take you very seriously. If you go to the bank with a half-baked, ill-conceived plan with nothing but enthusiasm behind it, then don't be surprised if you are shown the door, politely, of course.

Even the best business plan can meet with resistance. I well remember when I was about one year into my first company, I wanted to borrow ten thousand pounds for business expansion. I already had an established (but small) business. The first bank we went to looked over our (excellent) business plan and promptly said "good day". We were on the street before we knew what had hit us!

We were greatly discouraged, but we decided to try the bank next door. We were welcomed with open arms and congratulated on the thoroughness of our business plan. We were given the loan without question. The company still banks at this branch and has since put millions of pounds through the account!

The moral is that if you don't get any joy with your present bank, then try another.

I used to be scared of bank managers until I realised that I was the customer and THEY were there to serve me! I was doing them a favour by banking with them, even when I had a large overdraft, because that's how they make a lot of their money!

Let us assume that you find an agreeable bank manager who wants your business, the next problem comes with working capital.

Working Capital

This is the amount of money you will need to fund your business until it gets off the ground. In the window cleaning example, let us suppose that you only start to make money when you are cleaning at least five hundred windows a week. This means that for the first few months, you are going to be running at a loss. How are you going to fund that loss? The answer is with the money which you will be putting into the business to start with.

You will also need to buy quite a few items of 'capital' expenditure. For example a bike, ladders, buckets, typewriter, letterheads, leaflets, company registration fee, telephone answering machine and so on. This little lot can easily add up to a few thousand pounds; this is money going out the door before you get a penny back. Where are you going to get this money?

You can either fund it yourself, (from savings or by selling something), or you can borrow it.

If you are funding it yourself, your bank manager is likely to be very sympathetic to your cause because there is no risk to the bank – you are not asking for a loan or overdraft.

If, however, you are 'penniless' (remember my definition in chapter 6), then you will have to try and borrow the money from the bank.

In this case, your manager will go through your proposals with a fine tooth comb; even for a modest few thousand. In fact it has been my experience that the **larger** the amount you wish to borrow, the easier it is! The bank manager will also probably suggest that you match "pound for pound" any loan which is provided. For example, if you want £5000, it will be suggested that you put in £2500 and the bank puts in the other £2500. This has the effect of seeing how serious you are about your chances of success. If **you** aren't willing to back your brain-child with hard cash, then why should the bank be expected to have more faith in your idea than you do? At least, this is the bank's attitude. The fact that you haven't got a bean will cut little ice with them.

Also, don't expect to get any more than fiddling small change unless the loan is secured against a tangible asset (like your house). If you don't 'own' a house, then you are viewed as a miserably dis-advantaged lower life-form, and are most unlikely to be offered any loan worth having. If you are in this situation, then you will just have to find the money yourself somehow. I did.

Stationary

You will need to get some stationary printed. There are a few "Do's and Don'ts" concerning stationary; here they are:-

Your headed note-paper should contain your company name and trading address (normally at the top of the note-paper), your company's registered office address together with the names of the directors and the company registration number (usually in very small print along the bottom of the paper), and your phone/fax/telex number(s).

It is WELL WORTH WHILE getting your note-paper designed properly. There are a lot of companies who will do this for a very reasonable fee; otherwise your printer can organise something for you. DO NOT be tempted to try and 'Letraset' something yourself, unless you are particularly adept at this task. The result will give an overall shoddy impression, and even if *you* don't notice this sort of thing, believe me, other people do, and they will judge both you and your company on what they see.

Avoid using fancy type faces (Palace Script, for example, or 'thermo-relief', a process which gives a raised letter effect). Some people think that this looks good, or even professional, it doesn't!

Always use a reputable, small, jobbing printer to do your printing work. They are likely to do a first class job for you. Personally I would avoid the High Street "Quick Print" type of shop.

You will need the following lines of stationary as a minimum: letterheads, invoices, purchase orders and business cards. Depending upon the type of business, you may also need advertising leaflets etc.

Some small businesses use their letterheads for sending invoices and purchase orders, but this is false economy and looks amateurish.

Don't over-order! Unless you are sending out thousands of letters, you are most unlikely to need more than five hundred of each of the above items. This is a sensible, economic print run. Besides, you might change your address or company name.

Keeping Books

This is the number one golden, unbreakable rule for ALL businesses, particularly small ones:

KEEP GOOD, ACCURATE BOOKS

Without a doubt, this is the weakest area for most small businesses. There is no excuse for it. Book-keeping on this level is a snap! If you don't understand it, then there are dozens of excellent books which you can buy which will teach you, and it won't take long to learn, either.

If you really don't want to be bothered with this, then advertise for someone living locally to come in, say, one morning a week to do them for you; it won't cost a fortune and this will be the best money you ever spend.

The worst thing you can possibly do is to launch into your business without a proper book-keeping system installed, it will be a total shambles within a very short time; it will take months to unravel the mess and could cost you a lot of money.

It should take less than one day to install a system which will take you to a half million pound turnover and beyond; again, advertise for someone to set you up and explain it to you, it will be the best investment you ever made.

Be Professional

If you can hold this rule firmly in mind, you will not go too far wrong. You should aim to be strictly professional in every area of your business, for example:

The Job Itself: Every customer counts and is important. Never be tempted to write-off a customer as a nuisance, or "not worth bothering with." Always do a good, professional job and take pride in it, even if you lose money sometimes; believe me it will repay itself with huge dividends.

Once you start to slip into the 'cowboy' attitude then you are on a steeply sloping downward path to hack amateurism. Keep ALL of your customers satisfied, even if it means going to great lengths to ensure this.

Telephone: This is a major source of un-professionalism in even quite large companies who should know better.

Always answer the telephone in a positive cheerful manner; don't leave people hanging on and ALWAYS call people back when you say you will.

If you use a telephone answering machine, then get the recorded message done by someone with a good telephone manner. It is totally unforgivable to have an answering machine with a boring, amateur-sounding message, in the background of which can be heard a screaming baby!

Answer all messages promptly otherwise people will stop leaving them.

Stationary: This lets most small companies down. I have already pointed out the areas to watch, but do be careful of the small details – they matter.

Also watch your literacy. Very few people are as literate as they would like to think, and most people are very poor at spelling and grammar. There is nothing guaranteed to put a prospective customer off buying from your company than a letter or a piece of advertising which has a spelling or punctuation error. By the way, this is a classic I-CAN'T! ("I can't spell, I never have been able to, I'm useless at it!") Anyone can learn to spell to a high standard; and for words which still give trouble, there is always a dictionary!

Personal Visits: Look smart and professional at all times when visiting clients or VIPs. Even if you have chosen a job where you have to get your hands dirty then invest in several pairs of overalls with your company name monogrammed onto them; don't just turn up in your old gardening clothes.

Car/van: If you need to visit clients or customers regularly then buy the very best and most appropriate vehicle which you can afford. If this is a van, then get your company name painted on the side.

If you really cannot afford a decent company vehicle then park your own vehicle 'round the corner' when visiting clients. I had to do this for a few months before I could afford a vehicle worth parking in view of a client! Clients and customers judge the success of you and your business by the type of vehicle in which you arrive – rightly so. Don't expect to pick up a substantial order if you turn up in a ten year old Ford Cortina with a coat-hanger for an aerial and two large, orange furry-dice hanging from the mirror. Even if you are a jobbing plumber this would look very, very suspect. The customer would (rightly) wonder at the quality of your workmanship if your car was in such a poor state of repair.

Book-keeping: You must ensure that you keep accurate, neat records of your transactions. Believe me, you will experience severe problems if you don't. This applies *whatever* the size of the business. The smaller the business, the greater the temptation to muddle through somehow.

Your business life is going to be difficult enough without having the problems of messy financial records to contend with – get it right!

It's Up to You!

Now you are on your own. The next few years are going to involve you in a lot of hard work and effort. At times you will wonder whether it was all worth it! You will long for that quiet 'nine-to-five' existence which you gave up for more exciting ventures.

Gradually, however, the rewards of your efforts will start to come your way – a new car, a larger salary, freedom from the more mundane activities as you start to employ people, and many, many more benefits. From the very beginning you will have experienced one of the major benefits, that is the benefit of guiding your own destiny, of 'being at the helm of your own ship'.

This brings its own unique satisfaction and rewards.

Eventually, if all goes well, you will build the company up to a size where it could become of interest to a third party. The size at which you decide to sell depends upon the amount of money you wish to take, but it is not too difficult to make, say, a quarter of a million pounds from even a small company if the right buyer can be found.

If you are after a million (or more) then you will have to hang on much longer. It all depends on you. For example, you may enjoy the cut and thrust of business life so much that you are not anxious to sell too soon. You may be one of the many individuals who then take their company onto the stock market and make millions of pounds in the process. Don't forget that meanwhile, you will be enjoying the benefits of a senior executive – good salary, excellent car, expenses and so on.

Other Ways

Building a company and selling it is only one of the many ways of becoming extremely rich. There are many other ways.

It all depends upon your personal inclination. If you are inventive, then inventing something, patenting it and then selling it to a major company can make you extremely rich.

If you are artistic, then writing top-selling novels (and they really do have to sell a lot) or writing a hit song could provide you with a fortune in royalties over a good many years.

If you are interested in financial matters, then it is possible to make a fortune on the stock market. The newspapers recently reported a schoolboy who made a quarter of million pounds in his spare time. His stock-broker had not realised that he was under-age!

Choose something which you are good at. Don't say that you aren't particularly good at anything – that's an I-CAN'T excuse! Anyway, for every rich person who is a genius at their chosen profession, there are ten who are mediocre and yet BELIEVE in themselves.

I started this chapter by saying that it was the least important in the whole book. The next chapter, whilst the shortest, is probably the most important – read it carefully.

ETHICS

I consider this to be the most important chapter in the book, also the hardest to write.

This chapter is designed to serve as a warning. However, like all of the information which I have passed on to you in this book, I have no control over what you do with it after it has left my hands.

In the various chapters on PSI and I-CAN belief, I cautioned you against changing parts of the system to suite yourself; in fact I strongly advised you to follow my method to the letter. Obviously I have no control over whether you take my advice or not, I can only issue the warning and hope that you will listen to me.

Similarly, the contents of this short chapter are designed to warn you against certain courses of action. I really wrote this chapter for my own benefit since I could not, in all conscience, release the material in this book without including this chapter.

Use of The Method

The techniques which I have shared with you are extremely powerful, and like all things they could be used for good or bad. My first warning to you is as follows:

Do not use the methods contained in this book to harm or deprive other people. At all times be ethical in your use of the method.

An example of harming other people would be to use the method to gain promotion by actively visualising the person who was blocking your progress, meeting with an accident. Another example would be to use the method to increase your success rate in the burglaries which you were carrying out! There are also many more minor examples of the mis-use of this method.

If you ignore this warning then you will suffer accordingly. This is no dire threat on my behalf, but rather an immutable law. You may show some small gain initially, but believe me, you will lose eventually. You will also lose more than you gained in the first place, the net effect will be one pace forward and several large paces backwards.

At the very least, are you going to be happy in the future knowing that you obtained your wealth or status at the direct expense of other people? It could be argued that *any* wealth or status is obtained at the expense of other people, but then it can also be argued that apartheid is the only logical method of running a mixed-race country, or that six million Jews didn't really die in the last war. In all of these matters your conscience is quite capable of cutting through the intelectualisations and arriving at the truth of the matter.

Arthur Crook & Son

My second warning concerns the running of a shady business. The answer is – don't! Do not even be tempted into thinking that you are going to 'Get Rich Quick' by operating in some grey or even black area. There is only one way to run a business and that is straight down the line, being unscrupulously fair and honest with your customers. If you don't, then again you will suffer accordingly.

If nothing else, it's so much *easier* to run a straight business. You can concentrate your time, energy and talents on the company and not waste half of your time looking over your shoulder, keeping several different sets of accounts or fending off complaints from irate customers. Again, you may make some money to start off with, but it is very short lived. The only way to make money in the long term is to offer a service to your customers which they are happy to pay for, hopefully time and time again.

Few people reading this book have the intention of starting a child pornography ring, or running guns to Central America; such obvious evils are easy to spot by anyone with half a conscience. Yet a great many otherwise honourable people DO consider slightly shady areas of business. They wouldn't dream of cheating their next door neighbour, but a lot of gullible customers seem like fair game.

I define a shady business as one which does not give the customer genuine value for money, or is not soundly based enough to carry out the business advertised.

An example of a shady business is one which advertises a product or service which is not really available until a certain amount of money has been collected from customers replying to advertisements. This may be a company offering for sale a product (like an electronic mousetrap) and using the money sent in by the first thousand replies to actually fund the design of such a product, or keeping customer's money on deposit for three months to gain the interest, then sending it back with a letter explaining that the product is no longer available.

My publishers could have acted shadily by advertising this book, then when the response to the advert had been assessed, commissioning me to write it! I need hardly point out that we wrote the book first, had several thousand copies printed, *then* advertised it in the belief that it would sell. If it hadn't sold, *we* would have lost, not you. This is a golden rule in business; because it is YOU who stand to gain if your ideas work out as planned, it should be YOU who stand to lose if your ideas fall flat, NOT your customers – why should *they* fund your errors?

Other shady businesses involve selling low-priced items which are extremely poor value for money. The hope is that the customer will not bother to complain.

An example of this is the plethora of 'business guides' which clog the business columns of some newspapers. These 'guides' are usually three or four photocopied sheets of A4 paper, with badly typed information copied from a readily available book. They are usually sold for anything between three and ten pounds and are invariably 'written' by hack operators whose sole intention is to make money out of people's genuine desire for knowledge.

Even if these various shady schemes resulted in bumper profits (and they very rarely do), could you really live with yourself in the future if you got rich by one of these methods? It is not enough to say "let the buyer beware", but rather better to say "let the seller be fair".

I am well aware that these comments will not touch the heart of a hardened shady dealer; these people are like sharks in a fish pond and they care not one jot for the pain and misery which they might cause; getting rich is everything to them and they are totally unconcerned about the methods which they use to achieve their goals. I am aiming my comments at the 'normal' person who has the mistaken belief that all's fair in business. This is not so and you should aim to run YOUR business straight down the middle.

Mr.Tax-man

This includes the tax-man! "Surely," you would argue, "the tax-man is fair game, anything which can be clawed back from the Revenue, even dis-honestly, has got to be good?" Not so! The reason is that if you pursue this course, it diverts your attention away from the real business. You start keeping two sets of books, then worrying about hiding the second set! You lose several night's sleep if you are expecting a tax inspector to call, and you spend more time making your business appear legitimate on paper, than you do in actually running it!

Also, tax inspectors are far from stupid. They've seen it all before; your brilliant scheme for side-tracking cash from the company has only been done five hundred times before – this week! They are absolutely expert at looking through your books and picking up the tracks of your dis-honesty. They can ask some very awkward questions if you are totally honest; those questions become very hard to answer if you have been defrauding them. If you are honest (and they know if you are, or not) they will give you the benefit of the doubt over the odd genuine mistake they find in your books, but if they suspect that you are not playing fair, they will take your business apart line by line – it will then be up to YOU (not them) to prove that each item of expenditure going back to the year dot is genuine, and not a forgery on your part.

They particularly love small companies with a high cash turnover; I can't imagine why, but they seem to think that the proprietors of such companies will be tempted to side-track some of that cash into their own pockets! As if they would!

They use some pretty devious methods of catching you out as well.

I knew a man who ran a fish and chip shop; hardly the sort of business to attract a tax inspector, you might think, but that's just where you (and he) would be wrong. This sort of business is a prime target! This particular chip shop was very busy and popular and the owner was side-tracking about five hundred pounds every week into his back pocket. The tax people became suspicious when they did a routine inspection.

What aroused their suspicions? Well the owner had a wife who did not go out to work, and three children to support. He also had a new, good quality car, a brand-new caravan, and had recently returned from an expensive two week holiday. Nothing suspicious about this except that he claimed to be paying himself one hundred pounds a week; clearly only just enough to live on (if that), and certainly not enough to support his extravagent standard of living.

The inspectors mounted a three week watch on his premises and counted all the customers going in and out. They then raided the shop and checked the books; sure enough, only about half of the money had been entered. This man had been operating in this manner (getting greedier year by year) for over ten years. He had a lot of explaining to do, and a very, very large tax bill to pay. In cases like this, the Revenue tell YOU what they think you have stolen over the time period, and it is up to you to pay it, or prove conclusively that you have stolen less than this amount!

You may think that this man was small fry (if you'll pardon the pun) but look at it from the viewpoint of the Revenue. If they catch one man like this, then it makes ten thousand chip-shop owners around the country sit up and take notice. The increased tax revenue is far greater than they could get by catching one unique, large-scale tax fraudster, particularly as the latter villain will be an expert and far harder to catch and convict. One man like this can tie up a whole tax investigation team for years, whereas our chip-shop friend was a sitting target. Just for the record, chip-shop owners are not known to be any less honest than other business people!

Two other examples should amuse you: One chap was running a mail-order business from home, selling widgets. He received about ten percent of his money in cash, despite the fact that his advertisement stated that customers should not send cash through the post. He pocketed ALL of the cash and didn't put a single penny through the books. His first tax inspection proved his undoing, because he found it impossible to convince the inspector that not one single person over a two year period, had sent him a five pound note instead of a cheque or postal-order. The tax inspector estimated that twenty-five percent of people had done so (even though it was only ten percent), and our friend had to pay up! He would have been far cleverer if he had put *some* of the cash through, but even this won't save you as my next example shows:

Another chap running a mail-order business thought that tax-inspectors had the brains of chimpanzees, and that his master plan could outwit them all. His business received substantial amounts of cash from customers replying to mail-order advertisements. He processed about half of this cash in the normal way, the other half he side-tracked out of the business.

He went to great lengths to cover his tracks, eradicating the customers from his records once he had sent the goods, even keeping separate post-books. He dutifully banked the legitimate cash so that he could show the Revenue what a good boy he was being. He was duly inspected, and all seemed to be in order. Unknown to our friend however, the inspector had noticed that there were one or two funny things about the books.

First of all, the amount of cash banked was always about the same for three weeks out of four, regardless of the fact that the total income fluctuated week to week. In the fourth week (the last week of the month) the cash was always somewhat less. (This was because our friend started to get a bit short of money towards the end of each month, so he would take a little more out.)

Over the next few weeks, the tax office sent twenty fictitious orders for items advertised by our friend; in each case, the order was sent with cash. The addresses used were those of various clerks working at the tax office. All of the goods duly arrived, so the orders had obviously been processed by our friend, who was then duly raided! Surprise, surprise, only about six of the orders were shown on his books; no less than fourteen were missing! Fourteen out of twenty is seventy percent (he had been particularly greedy that month) and so the Revenue ordered him to pay tax on the missing seventy percent of cash sales since the start of his business!

In all of these matters, the tax inspector is looking for the correct *proportions* in the business. Despite the silly stories which circulate, they are not really interested in whether you claim three pounds a week or ten pounds a week to pay a cleaner, or even if the cleaner ever gets the money. They ARE interested in the proportion of petty cash which goes through the business in relation to the business as a whole. They ARE interested in how much you pay yourself, and are quite entitled to ask (and often do), how you manage on the money you claim to be paying yourself.

My advice is to play it absolutely one hundred percent honestly, anything else is just not worth the problems; you have more important things to do.

I hope that you will forgive my little excursion into morals; always a tricky subject at the best of times. My intention was to pass on my experience over many years of running businesses, small and large.